W9-ANM-896

SUCCESSFUL SCHOOL RESTRUCTURING

A Report to the Public and Educators
by the
Center on Organization and Restructuring of Schools

Fred M. Newmann and Gary G. Wehlage

Distributed jointly by the

American Federation of Teachers
Association for Supervision and Curriculum Development
National Association of Elementary School Principals
The National Association of Secondary School Principals

This is a progress report on findings that deserve serious attention by practicing educators, policymakers, researchers and the public at large. These findings should advance knowledge and educational practice.

At the same time, this summary is incomplete. The more detailed reports cited in notes offer a more complete treatment. This report's conclusions will be elaborated in future analyses to be summarized in the Center's final report, to be issued in 1996.

This report was prepared at the Center on Organization and Restructuring of Schools, supported by the U.S. Department of Education, Office of Educational Research and Improvement (Grant No. R117Q00005-95) and by the Wisconsin Center for Education Research, School of Education, University of Wisconsin-Madison. The opinions expressed in this publication are those of the authors and do not necessarily reflect the views of the supporting agencies.

Center on Organization and Restructuring of Schools
University of Wisconsin-Madison
School of Education
Wisconsin Center for Education Research
1025 W. Johnson Street
Madison, WI 53706
Telephone: (608) 263-7575

©Copyright 1995 by the Board of Regents of the University of Wisconsin System

The following organizations participated in the Center's National Advisory Panel. In order to maximize dissemination of this report, each of them has kindly agreed to assist with its distribution. To order copies contact any of the following:

American Federation of Teachers
Attention: AFT/Successful School
  Restructuring
555 New Jersey Avenue, N.W.
Washington, DC 20001
(prepayment required)

National Association of
  Elementary School Principals
Educational Products Division
1615 Duke Street
Alexandria, VA 22314-3483
800/386-2377

Association for Supervision and
  Curriculum Development
1250 N. Pitt Street
Alexandria, VA 22314-1453
800/933-2723

The National Association of
  Secondary School Principals
Attention: Publication Sales
1904 Association Drive
Reston, VA 22091
703/860-0200
800/253-7746

Price: $9.95

Table of Contents

List of Illustrations

Figures

Boxes

Acknowledgements

This report is the result of substantial collaborative effort among many researchers, who relied on the cooperation of students, their parents, teachers, and administrators in more than 1,500 schools throughout the United States. Because we have depended so much on the wisdom and hard work of others, we claim no exclusive credit for the ideas and findings articulated here. Since 1990, the Center's research has been advanced by 87 staff members, listed in the Appendix, who helped to plan the studies, collect the data, analyze and critique it, and write reports. The Center received insightful counsel from several external reviewers, from a distinguished National Advisory Panel (also listed in the Appendix) chaired by Richard Wallace, Jr., and from Ron Anson and other staff at Office of Educational Research and Improvement, the Center's main funding agency.

Space does not permit us to acknowledge everyone's specific contribution, but we owe a special debt to Anthony Bryk (University of Chicago), Valerie Lee (University of Michigan), and Karen Seashore Louis (University of Minnesota). The conclusions we report depend in immeasurable ways on their leadership of major studies in the Center, their powerful intellectual contributions, and their dedicated, enthusiastic collaboration.

Throughout this project Diane Randall provided superb administrative and technical support, along with a unique blend of judgment, sensitivity, and kindness that kept us together as a usually cheerful community.

OVERVIEW

The Problem

In 1983 Americans were warned in *A Nation at Risk* (National Commission on Excellence in Education) that a rising tide of mediocrity in their education system threatened the nation's security. Since then, the call to arms has centered on an arsenal of new tools to "restructure" schools. Restructuring has no precise definition, but the term suggests that schooling needs to be comprehensively redesigned; simply improving parts of schools as we know them isn't enough. Structural reforms include decentralization, shared decision-making, school choice, schools within schools, flexible scheduling with longer classes, teacher teaming, common academic curriculum required for all students, reduction of tracking and ability grouping, external standards for school accountability, and new forms of assessment, such as portfolios.

It is tempting to ask, Which reforms work the best for students? There is no simple answer to the question. Our studies of school restructuring indicate that, while each of these reforms has some potential to advance student learning, none of them, either alone or in combination, offers a sure remedy. The quality of education for children depends ultimately not on specific techniques, practices or structures, but on more basic human and social resources in a school, especially on the commitment and competence (the will and skill) of educators, and on students' efforts to learn.

In short, specific innovations should be seen as structural tools to be used for specific purposes in particular situations. Hammers, saws, or sandpaper can substantially enhance or diminish the value of the materials to which they are applied, but their effectiveness depends on how they are used in specific contexts. Similarly, the effectiveness of each education restructuring tool, either alone or in combination with others, depends on how well it organizes or develops the values, beliefs, and technical skills of educators to improve student learning.

Restructuring initiatives, by definition, introduce substantial departures from conventional practice. New configurations of power and authority challenge educators, students, and parents to perform new roles that require new skills and attitudes. The more that new practices and structural tools

1

depart from conventional practice, the greater the difficulties of implementation. Overcoming these difficulties, then, becomes a dominant concern of reformers, practitioners, and researchers. The prevailing issue often becomes, How do we implement the new practice or structural tool?

Although this question is reasonable, preoccupation with it often diverts attention from the more fundamental question: How is the new structural tool or practice likely to improve our school's human and social resources to increase student learning?

The "Solution"

Starting with a focus on student learning, the point of our research was to learn how the tools of restructuring can be used to elevate learning for all students. There is no "magic bullet" or simple recipe for success. But the solution lies in the "circles of support," diagrammed in Figure 1.

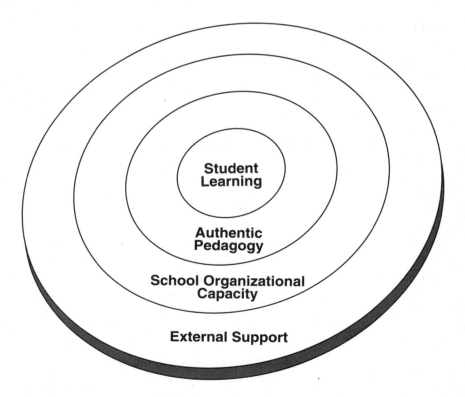

Figure 1: Circles of Support–The Context for Successful School Restructuring.

1. Student Learning. Planning, implementation, and evaluation must focus on how current practice and innovation enhance the intellectual quality of student learning. Teachers in schools need to agree on a vision of high quality intellectual work. Goals for high quality learning need to be communicated to students and parents. Curriculum, instruction, assessment, scheduling, staff development, hiring, student advising—all the core activities of the school— must be oriented toward the vision of student learning. The Center on Organization and Restructuring of Schools (CORS) developed a particular vision of high quality student learning called authentic student achievement. We found that when schools restructure around this kind of vision, it works— students learn more.

2. Authentic Pedagogy. A vision for high quality student learning is a necessary guide, but not sufficient. Teachers must teach according to the vision. What kind of teaching promotes high quality learning? To address this question, CORS developed teaching standards, not to prescribe techniques such as cooperative learning or portfolios, but to gauge the intellectual quality of the pedagogy we observed; that is, the mix of activities and interaction that teachers use to instruct and assess students.

Our standards emphasize teaching that requires students to think, to develop in-depth understanding, and to apply academic learning to important, realistic problems. We call this "authentic pedagogy," and we found that authentic pedagogy boosted student achievement equitably for students of all social backgrounds.

3. School Organizational Capacity. Learning of high intellectual quality is difficult work for students, and authentic pedagogy places complex, demanding challenges on teachers. How can schools be organized to help them meet these challenges? The solution here is not only to hire or train competent staff, but to build the capacity of the school to work well as a unit that strives for continuous improvement. The most successful schools were those that used restructuring tools to help them function as professional communities. That is, they found a way to channel staff and student efforts toward a clear, commonly shared purpose for student learning; they created opportunities for teachers to collaborate and help one another achieve the purpose; and teachers in these schools took collective—not just individual—responsibility for student learning. Schools with strong professional communities were better able to offer authentic pedagogy and were more effective in promoting student achievement.

4. External Support. Schools are nested in a complex environment of expectations, regulations, and professional stimulation from external sources including districts, state and federal agencies, independent reform projects, parents and other citizens. Schools need critical financial, technical, and political support from these external sources. We found that external agencies helped schools to focus on student learning and to enhance organizational capacity through three strategies: setting standards for learning of high intellectual quality; providing sustained, schoolwide staff development; and using deregulation to increase school autonomy. But sometimes external influences pulled schools in different directions, imposed unreasonable regulations, and instigated rapid shifts in policy and leadership, all of which can undermine organizational capacity.

In brief, we found that restructuring offered no panacea, but that it advanced student learning when it concentrated on the intellectual quality of student work, when it built schoolwide organizational capacity to deliver authentic pedagogy, and when it received support from the external environment that was consistent with these challenges. This report is organized around these circles of support, since they are what makes restructuring work for students, rather than around specific restructuring initiatives such as site-based management or flexible scheduling.

The Research

What kinds of schools did we study as examples of restructuring? As suggested above, we used "restructuring" to represent no single change or set of changes, but we considered each of the following to be important examples:

- site-based management and shared decision-making, with the school having meaningful authority over staffing, school program, and budget;

- students and teachers organized into teams responsible for most of students' instruction, with frequent common planning time for teachers;

- students participating in multiyear instructional or advisory groups;

- students grouped heterogeneously for instruction in the core subjects;

- enrollment based on student and parent choice rather than residential location.

With these multiple factors, it is more useful to think of schools as restructuring to a greater or lesser extent, rather than as categorically restructured or conventional. And restructuring occurs both when existing schools make major changes and when new schools are established to implement factors like these.

Box 1

SOURCES OF EVIDENCE

School Restructuring Study (SRS). This study included 24 significantly restructured public schools, evenly divided among elementary, middle, and high schools, located in 16 states and 22 districts, mostly in urban settings. There was a large range of enrollment, with an average of 777 students; 21 percent African American; 22 percent Hispanic; 37 percent receiving free or reduced lunch. From 1991 through 1994 each school was studied intensively for one year during two weeks of on-site research. Narrative reports were supplemented by surveys of students and staff, conventional tests of student achievement, and the scoring of student achievement on two teacher-assigned assessments according to standards of authentic performance. Researchers also made intensive study of mathematics and social studies instruction in about 130 classrooms, with complete data on about 2,000 students. This study allowed intensive examination of authentic pedagogy and student performance in a carefully selected group of schools that had made significant progress in restructuring.[1]

National Educational Longitudinal Study of 1988 (NELS:88). This study included a nationally representative sample of over 10,000 students, followed from grade 8 (1988) through grade 12 (1992) in about 800 high schools nationwide. The schools include public, Catholic, and independent schools and represent a wide range of school enrollment, geographic settings, school social composition, as well as various levels of restructuring activity. Student test data in mathematics, science, reading and history for grades 8, 10, and 12 were drawn from items from the National Assessment of Educational Progress. Researchers also studied survey data from teachers and students, and the school principal's report on curriculum, instruction, school climate, and the extent of school restructuring. Complementing the more intensive study of school restructuring in the SRS, this study permitted examination of factors that influence student learning on conventional achievement tests over four years of high school in a large representative national sample of secondary schools and students.[2]

Study of Chicago School Reform. This study included survey data from 8,000 teachers and principals in 400 elementary and 40 high schools from 1990 to 1994. Surveys reported on instruction, school climate and organizational features, professional activities, relations with parents, and reform activities. The study also included three-year case studies of 12 elementary schools, including six schools actively involved in restructuring. Case study schools represent the full range of elementary schools in Chicago, which vary substantially in social composition, but most have a majority of poor and minority children. The study, focusing on local school politics and school organizational change, offered both in-depth case analysis and extensive quantitative information on the nation's most ambitious effort in school decentralization.[3]

Longitudinal Study of School Restructuring. This study included four-year case studies of eight schools that had embarked on different forms of restructuring in four communities. Representing a variety of school social composition and enrollment, the schools included two urban elementary schools, two urban middle schools, two urban high schools, and a rural middle school and high school. From 1991 through 1994, researchers spent about 15 person-days per year in observations and interviews at each school, studying teachers' work, interactions in groups, participation in decision-making and organizational learning. The study offered in-depth analysis of how professional community, politics and organizational learning evolved in a diverse set of restructured schools.[4]

This report synthesizes findings of research conducted by CORS staff from 1990 through 1995. Research on educational reform poses complex problems, which call for diverse research designs and methodologies. Our conclusions are drawn primarily from four projects described in Box 1.

These studies provided a rich combination of in-depth case studies, along with survey data that portray general trends. They included schools at different stages of restructuring that participated in a variety of district and state reform strategies, including public school choice, radical decentralization, and state level systemic reform.

I.
STUDENT LEARNING

T he central goal of school is student learning, and the purpose of learning is to promote students' cognitive development. A strong intellectual focus for student learning is critical to meet modern society's demands for more complex cognitive functioning in order to prepare students for further schooling or for work. But keen use of the mind is also important for competent participation in democratic civic life, for emotional development, and for efficient management of personal affairs.

We would expect school restructuring to focus educators' attention on the knowledge and intellectual skills they want students to master. Observing staff meetings and daily lessons, we would expect to hear sustained dialogue about what content, skills, and dispositions are most important to teach. We would hope to hear teachers explain how knowledge from different disciplines can be used to enrich the meaning of students' daily experience. In classrooms, we would hope to hear students supporting their statements with reason and with the best available knowledge from a relevant discipline. When concerns of this sort permeate dialogue among staff and students, we recognize that a central priority for the school is high quality student learning.

But how do we know when students have learned to use their minds well— rigorously and creatively?

In a high school interdisciplinary mathematics and science class that we observed, students designed rides for an amusement park, after visiting a nearby park and taking several rides.[5] The assignment required students to calculate dimensions of their rides, the size of the carriers, the number of people who could reasonably go on the ride at the same time, the means of locomotion, and the materials that were needed. If a ride moved passengers at high speed, the velocity had to be calculated to determine practicality and safety. Does having students produce this kind of performance demonstrate learning of high intellectual quality? If so, what criteria can be used to judge how proficient a particular student's performance might be?

To answer these questions, CORS developed standards for student performance and for teaching that facilitates student performance of high intellectual quality. The specific standards, explained later, come from a general vision of high quality achievement.[6]

Authentic Adult Achievement: A Foundation for Standards

How do we recognize significant human accomplishments that involve skilled intellectual work? Consider the task of designing a bridge. Successful completion of this task illustrates some of the essential intellectual qualities of authentic achievement. Typically, the work requires using both new and well-established knowledge in the fields of design and construction. New knowledge is produced as special conditions are addressed involving the bridge's particular length, height, peak points of stress and load, and also the impact of possible environmental conditions involving weather extremes of temperature, wind, ice, snow, and floods, as well as the possibility of earthquakes. Disciplines of engineering, architecture, various natural sciences, and mathematics have accumulated bodies of reliable knowledge and procedures for solving the more routine problems of bridge design. However, problems unique to each setting will require new conceptions of design and construction. When completed, the bridge will be safe and useful to travelers. It may also make a significant aesthetic statement, and it will likely be considered a personally satisfying accomplishment to those who designed it.

Significant adult accomplishments, such as designing a bridge, reflect three criteria that can be used to assess the intellectual quality of student achievement as well: **construction of knowledge, disciplined inquiry, and value beyond school.** Adults in diverse fields face the primary challenge of constructing or producing meaning or knowledge. They construct knowledge through disciplined inquiry that uses knowledge, skills, and technology. They express the results of this disciplined inquiry in written, symbolic, and oral discourse, by making things (products such as furniture, bridges, videos, or sculpture), and in performances for audiences (musical, dramatic, or athletic). These expressions and products have value beyond success in school; that is, they have aesthetic, utilitarian, or personal value to the persons constructing them and to others in the society.

Construction of Knowledge

When students construct knowledge, they organize, synthesize, interpret, explain, or evaluate information. To do this well, they must build on prior knowledge that others have produced. As they assimilate prior knowledge, they should hone their skills through guided practice in producing original conversation and writing, through building physical objects, or through artistic and musical performances.

However, conventional curriculum excessively emphasizes reproducing knowledge: memorizing algorithms to solve routine mathematics problems, for example, or naming the different functions of parts of speech, or matching authors with titles and explorers with their feats. The mere reproduction of prior knowledge does not constitute authentic academic achievement, because it does not involve the thoughtful use or application of knowledge found in authentic adult accomplishment.

Disciplined Inquiry

A second defining feature of authentic achievement is its reliance on disciplined inquiry. Disciplined inquiry is complex cognitive work, because it integrates at least three important intellectual activities.

First, disciplined inquiry uses an established knowledge base; that is, it employs the facts, concepts, and theories that other inquirers have provided. Second, disciplined inquiry strives for an in-depth understanding of problems; superficial acquaintance with knowledge is inadequate to solve problems. In contrast, conventional schoolwork dwells mainly on transmitting prior knowledge—the first part of disciplined inquiry. Schoolwork rarely helps students develop in-depth understanding through which they can explore issues, relationships, and complexities within focused, limited topics.

Third, scientists, jurists, artists, journalists, designers, engineers, and other inquirers working within disciplines elaborate on their ideas and findings both orally and in writing. The language they use—verbal, symbolic, and visual—includes qualifications, nuances, elaborations, details, and analogues woven into extended expositions, narratives, explanations, justifications, and dialogue. But much of the communication demanded in school asks only for brief responses: choosing true or false, selecting from multiple choices, filling in blanks, or writing short sentences (e.g., "Prices increase when demand exceeds supply.")

In-depth understanding and elaborated communication may appear too sophisticated for children to grasp. But we take the position, supported by many educators and psychologists and evidenced by the success of several teachers we observed, that all students are capable of engaging in these forms of cognitive work when the work is adapted to students' levels of development.

Value Beyond School

Finally, authentic human achievements have aesthetic, utilitarian, or personal value apart from documenting the competence of the learner. When adults write letters, news articles, scientific papers, or poems, design buildings, create paintings or music or build furniture, they are trying to communicate ideas, produce products, or have an impact on others beyond simply demonstrating that they are competent. Achievements of this sort have a value that is missing in tasks contrived only for the purpose of assessing knowledge (such as quizzes,

Box 2

STANDARDS FOR AUTHENTIC STUDENT PERFORMANCE

Construction of Knowledge

Standard 1: Analysis

Mathematics: Student performance demonstrates thinking with mathematical content by organizing, synthesizing, interpreting, hypothesizing, describing patterns, making models or simulations, constructing mathematical arguments, or inventing procedures.

Social Studies: Student performance demonstrates higher order thinking with social studies content by organizing, synthesizing, interpreting, evaluating, and hypothesizing to produce comparisons, contrasts, arguments, application of information to new contexts, and consideration of different ideas or points of view.

Disciplined Inquiry

Standard 2: Disciplinary Concepts

Mathematics: Student performance demonstrates an understanding of important mathematical ideas that goes beyond application of algorithms by elaborating on definitions, making connections to other mathematical concepts, or making connection to other disciplines.

Social Studies: Student performance demonstrates an understanding of ideas, concepts, theories, and principles from social disciplines and civic life by using them to interpret and explain specific, concrete information or events.

Standard 3: Elaborated Written Communication

Mathematics: Student performance demonstrates a concise, logical, and well-articulated explanation or argument that justifies mathematical work.

Social Studies: Student performance demonstrates an elaborated account that is clear and coherent and provides richness in details, qualifications and argument. The standard could be met by elaborated consideration of alternative points of view.

Value Beyond School

Not applicable in this study. See discussion on page 11.

laboratory exercises, or final exams). Authenticity calls for student accomplishments to have value beyond simply showing the teacher, the parent, a college, or an employer that the student has mastered the requirements of schooling.

The three criteria—construction of knowledge, through disciplined inquiry, to produce discourse, products, and performances that have meaning beyond success in school—define authentic achievement. While all three criteria are essential, a given achievement can be high on one criterion and lower on others.

But in school, as in life, one would not expect all activities to meet all three standards all of the time. For example, repetitive practice, retrieving information, and memorization of facts or rules may be necessary to build knowledge and skills as a foundation for authentic performance, or even to prepare students for the less authentic tests required by the current educational system. The point is not to abandon all forms of less authentic work in school, but to keep authentic achievement clearly in view as the ideal, valued end.

Standards for Authentic Student Performance

We use criteria for authentic adult achievement to set specific standards for the quality, success, or proficiency of student performance. The standards presented here are derived from two of the three general criteria of authenticity—construction of knowledge and disciplined inquiry. They require students to show successful analysis, understanding of disciplinary concepts, and elaborated communication. Specific standards for mathematics and social studies are presented in Box 2.

It was impractical for us to collect useful information on the value of student performances beyond the classroom, the third criterion for authentic achievement. Making judgments about the meaning or value of each student's performance, either to the student or to others beyond school, is theoretically possible, but it would have required interviews, surveys, or other ways of assessing the actual impact of the students' work. We simply did not have the resources and opportunity to do this. Instead, we judged whether the teachers' assessment tasks posed problems that had significance beyond school and whether the tasks demanded communication with audiences beyond school.

Students' written work met the criterion of construction of knowledge to the extent it demonstrated **analysis.** For example, in the mathematics/science activity described above, in which students designed an amusement park ride, one girl chose to design a water ride. Her final report specified the shape and construction of a boat made of balsa wood. She explained in writing that her choice of balsa was based on the relative cost of other materials. Her computations supported her claims that the ride was practical (it would float when carrying a passenger of 180 pounds). In doing her calculations, she employed the formula for density involving volume and mass. This work was judged high on analysis by experienced mathematics teachers who applied the CORS standards to samples of student work.

Students' work met the criterion of disciplined inquiry to the extent it demonstrated knowledge and use of **disciplinary concepts** and appropriate **elaborated written communication.** For example, a fifth-grade social studies class had been studying the relationship between environmental problems and the quality of human life. One student submitted a paper entitled "Overpopulation," from which we offer a few excerpts:

> Demography is the study of populations. Demographers study the populations of communities and countries. Demographers tell us about population statistics and the social, economic, and health characteristics of people. These studies can help us decide if we are overpopulated.

> Most people don't understand how overpopulated we are. Experts say that you can't have five minutes of silence without hearing some kind of man-made machine. . . . If overpopulation keeps happening, we will begin to run out of clean air and water, our natural resources will get used up, and we will lose our food supply. . . .

> Although most population experts agree that overpopulation is bad, not all agree we are overpopulated. . . . Garret Hardin estimated that the world could feed 300 billion people. Right now we have a world population of "only" 6 billion. . . .

> Overpopulation has many fatal effects. It can result in people losing their jobs and in homelessness, hunger, and getting disease. In some places like Ethiopia and Somalia where there is famine, there is so little food that terrorists steal for themselves. . . . Overpopulation can also lead to under-population. Studies of animals prove this. Wolves hunt hares. If the hare population rises, that means the wolf population rises, because now they have more food . . . but the wolf doesn't conserve food. He'll just eat away, and when the hares die out, the wolf population begins to die out. . . .

This student's report provided an elaborated analysis and discussion of the concept of overpopulation. It used disciplinary concepts from demography that relate population to economic and social conditions. It also showed some understanding of a theoretical model from biology involving the interaction of wolf and hare populations. The report presented not only sufficient factual knowledge, but also important qualifications and limitations of experts' under-standing of the topic.

These examples illustrate performances of high intellectual quality, but the question remains: How can schools help students produce these kinds of intellectual accomplishments? In the next sections, we present standards for teaching that can promote authentic student performance.

II.
AUTHENTIC PEDAGOGY

How can teachers help students produce authentic performance of high intellectual quality? Can we translate our vision of authentic achievement into practical classroom strategies for the teacher?

Teachers communicate what is important to learn through two main activities: the tests or other tasks they use to assess student mastery, and the instruction they conduct to help students prepare for the assessments. Together, the two parts of teaching practice are considered "pedagogy." From our vision of authentic adult achievement, we developed a set of standards to judge the intellectual quality of teachers' pedagogy; that is, their assessment tasks and instruction. Later in this section, we will present findings, indicating that pedagogy meeting these standards of intellectual quality leads to more authentic student performance.

Authentic Assessment Tasks

In the School Restructuring Study (SRS), we considered only tasks calling for written work because, at the very least, all students should learn to write well in both mathematics and social studies and because we were not prepared to evaluate other kinds of products and performances that might meet standards of authenticity. Box 3 presents the standards for assessment tasks.

Construction of Knowledge

A task calls for construction of knowledge if it asks students to **organize information** and to **consider alternatives.** For example, an eighth-grade teacher asked her students to write a report comparing immigration past and present:

> Immigration has occurred throughout American history. Identify major groups of people entering this country and indicate when most of them came. What events or conditions motivated these different groups to immigrate to the United States? How has immigration been regulated and controlled? How has regulation changed over time? Why is immigration now a major issue in this country? In what ways is the issue the same or different now?

Box 3

STANDARDS FOR AUTHENTIC PEDAGOGY: ASSESSMENT TASKS

Construction of Knowledge

Standard 1: Organization of Information. The task asks students to organize, synthesize, interpret, explain, or evaluate complex information in addressing a concept, problem, or issue.

Standard 2: Consideration of Alternatives. The task asks students to consider alternative solutions, strategies, perspectives, or points of view in addressing a concept, problem, or issue.

Disciplined Inquiry

Standard 3: Disciplinary Content. The task asks students to show understanding and/or to use ideas, theories, or perspectives considered central to an academic or professional discipline.

Standard 4: Disciplinary Process. The task asks students to use methods of inquiry, research, or communication characteristic of an academic or professional discipline.

Standard 5: Elaborated Written Communication. The task asks students to elaborate on their understanding, explanations, or conclusions through extended writing.

Value Beyond School

Standard 6: Problem Connected to the World Beyond the Classroom. The task asks students to address a concept, problem, or issue that is similar to one that they have encountered or are likely to encounter in life beyond the classroom.

Standard 7: Audience Beyond the School. The task asks students to communicate their knowledge, present a product or performance, or take some action for an audience beyond the teacher, classroom, and school building.

This task was scored high on "organization of information" because it required students to gather and synthesize information about immigrant groups, to make distinctions among them, to generalize about causal conditions in different historical periods, and, finally, to indicate why immigration is a contemporary issue. The task did not score as high on "consideration of alternatives" because it did not explicitly require students to compare alternative immigration policies (although we can imagine adding this to the task).

In an eighth-grade mathematics class, students were instructed to build a set of polyhedrons, known as the Platonic Solids or regular polyhedrons:

> The simplest Platonic Solid can be assembled out of four congruent equilateral triangles and is called a regular tetrahedron or a regular triangular pyramid. Your job is to build this and all other possible regular polyhedrons.

> Make a chart showing which shapes you use, how many faces your polyhedron has, and how many faces meet at each vertex. Also note any attempts or strategies that proved impossible. . . .

> Finally, explain in paragraph form why a limited number of regular polyhedrons are possible to make with each shape. Imagine that you are writing to seventh-graders whose only knowledge of polyhedrons is this set of directions. Think of how you can explain the possibilities and limitations. Include drawings and diagrams that might be helpful.

The CORS staff scored this task high on both "organization of information" and "consideration of alternatives." The task could be completed successfully only if students organized information to consider alternative shapes and how these shapes would or would not fit the geometric definition of a Platonic polyhedron. To arrive at mathematically accurate conclusions, students had to consider the methods or strategies for building the polyhedrons and explanations for why there are a limited number of possibilities, and they had to choose appropriate phrasing to make their explanations understandable to a younger student.

Disciplined Inquiry

A task calls on students to engage in disciplined inquiry if it requires understanding of **disciplinary content,** requires students to use a **process** common to disciplinary inquiry, and if it requires **elaborated communication.**

For example, fifth-graders were asked to "draw geometric designs of your own making on a grid. Write a BASIC program that will replicate these designs." This task rated high on disciplinary content because it required students to understand the relationship between aspects of Cartesian geometry and algorithmic processes in mathematics.

Another group of fifth-graders was given the following problem: "If a 12-toothed gear turns one time, how many times would each of these gears turn: 2-toothed gear, 3-toothed gear, and 4-toothed gear? Explain how to find the number of turns that a gear will take when connected to another gear." This task scored high on mathematical disciplinary process because it required discovering the relationship of wheel turns to the number of teeth. In explaining the relationship, students would need to create conventions for writing about ratios and proportions.

Value Beyond School

A task fulfills the third criterion, value beyond the school, to the extent it meets two standards: one calls for students to address a **problem likely to be encountered beyond school,** and the second asks that students communicate their findings or message to an **audience beyond the classroom.**

Fourth-graders who had been studying ecology were given the following assignment:

> Write a letter to a state assembly representative or state senator expressing your opinion about what should be done about threatened eagles along the Mississippi River. Your letter should be persuasive and it should also do the following:
>
>> Communicate knowledge about the subject.
>>
>> Organize ideas into paragraphs.
>>
>> Begin sentences in different ways.
>>
>> Use dialogue to communicate ideas.
>>
>> Use correct letter format.
>>
>> Use correct punctuation and spelling.
>
> Ask a peer to read your letter and offer constructive criticism. When your are satisfied with your letter, send it.

This task challenged students to meet a number of the seven standards of intellectual quality for tasks. They had to organize information to address a problem, communicate knowledge and opinion effectively, and address their communication to an actual audience beyond the school in an attempt to produce influence on a public issue.

Authentic Instruction

What kind of instruction will help students succeed when confronted with authentic tasks that meet the standards described above? Student-centered practices such as discussions, small-group work, and hands-on projects are usually assumed to provide more authentic experiences for children. We found, however, that many activities of this sort do not necessarily support construction of knowledge, disciplined inquiry, or learning that has application beyond school. Whether "teacher centered" (e.g., teacher-directed discussion) or "student centered" (e.g., cooperative learning), instruction should be designed to promote the three main qualities of authentic achievement.

We developed four standards to assess instruction according to the criteria for authentic academic achievement. The specific standards are presented in Box 4. The first three—higher order thinking, deep knowledge, and substantive conversation—place special emphasis on cognitive complexity, or what some call "teaching for conceptual understanding." The fourth standard, connections to the world beyond the classroom, emphasizes teaching that helps students apply such understanding in contexts beyond school that are often considered more authentic.[7]

Box 4

STANDARDS FOR AUTHENTIC PEDAGOGY: INSTRUCTION

Construction of Knowledge

Standard 1. Higher Order Thinking: Instruction involves students in manipulating information and ideas by synthesizing, generalizing, explaining, hypothesizing, or arriving at conclusions that produce new meaning and understandings for them.

Disciplined Inquiry

Standard 2. Deep Knowledge: Instruction addresses central ideas of a topic or discipline with enough thoroughness to explore connections and relationships and to produce relatively complex understandings.

Standard 3. Substantive Conversation: Students engage in extended conversational exchanges with the teacher and/or their peers about subject matter in a way that builds an improved and shared understanding of ideas or topics.

Value Beyond School

Standard 4. Connections to the World Beyond the Classroom: Students make connections between substantive knowledge and either public problems or personal experiences.

Teachers help students "construct knowledge" when they engage students in **higher order thinking.** For example, a fifth-grade mathematics teacher challenged students to estimate answers to a series of increasingly more complex multiplication problems. She provided no instructions, procedures, or clues on how to do this. Working in groups, students developed their own insights and rules for how to solve estimation problems, and the teacher constantly challenged them to explain their thinking.

Instruction that helped students acquire **deep knowledge** facilitated disciplined inquiry. For example, a social studies teacher wanted students to gain an in-depth understanding of the concept of culture. She had the students use and elaborate on the concept by studying different groups from different perspectives. In one extended lesson, students compared the housing of early Native Americans: the Pueblo of the Southwest, the Kwakiutl of the Northwest coast, the Iroquois in what is now New York, and the Algonquin in what is now Ontario. Students found that different environments provided very different building materials, including stone and mud, wood, and animal skins. The lesson led students to notice that the physical environment provided resources for different housing styles. Students also discovered that customs and values produced different living arrangements; both communal and single-family dwellings were found among Native Americans.

Disciplined inquiry is promoted through **substantive conversation.** This kind of talk occurs when students are engaged in extended exchanges with a teacher or peers that builds an improved and shared understanding of a topic. For example, some students in the high school mathematics/physics class that designed amusement park rides were asked by the teacher to consider the height of their own proposed ride (125 meters). What velocity would a rider have at the bottom of such a fall? Would the speed be reasonable? Initially, the students saw no problem with the ride. The teacher asked them to consider the height of the ride they had seen at the amusement park; it measured 14 meters. Students discussed acceleration and determined that their own 125-meter fall would be unsafe. Additionally, the students discussed the effects of curving the track of a free-fall; a ride would immediately begin to decelerate on a curve. The students discussed relationships among acceleration, velocity, deceleration, and the amount of time and distance needed to bring the ride to a safe stop.

The third general criterion for authenticity calls on instruction to make **connections to the world beyond the classroom.** Teachers help students see the relationship between classroom learning and issues or topics outside the school. For example, in a high school history class, students explored the causes of World War I. Their teacher guided a class discussion to help students recognize parallels between conditions of 1914 that led to that war and more recent troubles involving Serbs, Croats, and Bosnian Muslims. Through their discussion, students expressed concern that the similarities in contemporary conditions might lead much of Europe into another war.

How the Standards Can Help Teachers, Students, and Schools

The standards for authentic pedagogy and performance were developed initially as a research tool for examining intellectual quality in restructuring schools. After refining them over several years, we think they can help teachers, students, and schools define more clearly what constitutes high quality intellectual work.

But we do not recommend the standards as a recipe to be literally adopted and implemented. The intellectual quality of education will not be enhanced by mechanistic adoption of any specific short-term innovation. Instead, we propose the standards as a vehicle to steer the conversation about reform away from the logistics, management, and politics of new techniques and toward the intellectual quality we seek in classrooms. It will require years of sustained focus on the issue of intellectual quality of student learning to infuse standards like these into the culture of schools.[8]

We present the standards in the spirit of debate and experimentation and to further clarify the practical meaning of high intellectual standards for pedagogy and student performance. In their present form, the standards can stimulate reflection about the quality of student learning in schools. Small groups of teachers and departments and even whole schools can use the standards to reflect on their pedagogy.

One scenario is for teachers to score and discuss each other's instruction to determine the extent to which they are providing students with authentic cognitive challenges. Teachers also can collect examples of their assessment tasks and student performance and then rate the extent to which tasks are helping students to construct knowledge, engage in disciplined inquiry, and produce work that has value beyond the classroom. While these standards were developed only for mathematics and social studies, teachers in other subjects can discuss their appropriateness for other disciplines and modify them if necessary.

The Center's standards for authentic intellectual work are silent about the specific content students should be expected to learn in any subject or grade level. It remains to be seen whether meaningful content standards can be developed and broadly accepted in U.S. schools. We think some worthwhile content can and should be specified for various subjects and grade levels, but there is far too much worthwhile knowledge for all children to learn. Selecting some knowledge as more important than other knowledge, and requiring it for all children in a democratic nation, is difficult. Even the "knowledge experts" disagree about what should be required learning. Ultimately, the people have a right to help decide this issue.

Whether specific content standards originate primarily from local schools, districts, states, or professional organizations, we think the kinds of standards advanced here are necessary to help content standards promote intellectual quality. Without standards of the type we suggest, there is a strong possibility that content standards will continue to encourage mindless coverage of superficial, isolated bits of knowledge.

Moreover, if standard-setting comes to mean that each subject develops a unique set of content to be taught, teachers of different subjects will have no common intellectual standards for assessing school success. The lack of a common language for standards across grade levels, subjects, and departments impedes the development of schoolwide vision that, as we show in Section III, is important for promoting intellectual quality. The CORS standards, while placing a major emphasis on disciplinary content, avoid an exclusive focus on specific content standards, which has the potential to "balkanize" schools. The standards of intellectual quality presented here have the added benefit of providing a common language with which educators, parents, and the general public can talk to one another about learning and performance, regardless of subjects or grade levels.[9]

Finally, our standards of intellectual quality respect diversity in teaching style. Authentic instruction can occur in both "teacher-centered" and "student-centered" classrooms. Techniques such as small group discussions and cooperative learning might rate high or low on authentic pedagogy. Similarly, classes that were highly structured might rate high or low on the standards.

No particular vision of classroom structure, such as the "open classroom," is implied by the standards. Educators can use standards such as these to assess progress toward intellectual quality within a variety of teaching techniques and classroom structures.

Authentic Pedagogy Boosts Achievement for All Students

We used the standards for authentic pedagogy to gauge the level of student learning promoted in restructuring schools. We were particularly interested in whether authentic pedagogy provided equal opportunity to learn; that is, whether it helped students from all social backgrounds equally, or if it magnified inequalities in achievement between groups that traditionally have been more and less advantaged.

We examined these issues in two studies. The School Restructuring Study (SRS) of 24 elementary, middle, and high schools involved in-depth on-site analysis and the scoring of student performance according to our standards for authentic student performance. CORS also analyzed the National Educational Longitudinal Study of 1988 (NELS:88), which relied primarily on survey data from teachers and students in about 800 high schools nationwide. Its measure of student performance consisted of conventional multiple-choice items in mathematics and science.

Each study had advantages and disadvantages. The SRS involved multiple observations of teaching practice and student performance in carefully selected elementary, middle, and high schools that had made significant progress in restructuring, and it entailed systematic application of our standards for authentic pedagogy. But this study collected data during only one year at each school and did not track student performance over time. The NELS study, while only of high schools, included a large sample of schools that reported minimal to substantial restructuring practices, and it tracked student achievement over four years. But NELS contained only survey measures of authentic instruction, which were not entirely aligned with the standards of authentic pedagogy articulated above.[10] Together, however, the two studies give information on the contribution of authentic pedagogy to student achievement, when measured according to both authentic and conventional notions of school performance.

SRS Results

All schools in the SRS demonstrated clear progress in organizational restructuring, but they varied substantially in their success on the standards for authentic pedagogy.[11] In some schools, our researchers found many examples of high quality authentic practice in both mathematics and social studies. In others, however, they found few examples in either subject. If we assume that our standards of intellectual quality are appropriate goals, then there is good news and bad news. The good news is that some teachers and schools have been reasonably successful, signaling hope that authentic pedagogy is achievable. The bad news is that overall levels of authentic pedagogy remain low according to these standards, even in highly restructured schools, and that some teachers and schools have barely begun the journey toward authentic pedagogy.

This variability is important, because the level of authentic pedagogy affects student learning. Combining the results for students in mathematics and

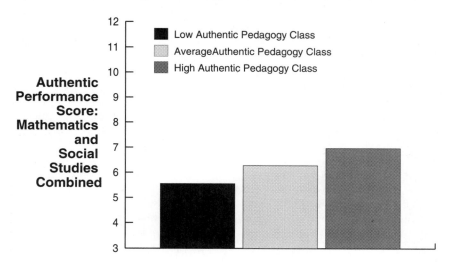

Figure 2: Level of Authentic Student Performance for Students Who Experience Low, Average, and High Authentic Pedagogy in Restructuring Elementary, Middle, and High Schools. (See Note 12.)

social studies, we found that authentic pedagogy boosts the academic performance of students at all three grade levels in both mathematics and social studies.

Figure 2 shows the performance consequences of low, medium, and high authentic pedagogy for hypothetical average students.[12] Although these increments in raw test scores may seem small when compared to the absolute scale of 3 to 12 points, they reflect substantial improvements in these students' authentic academic performance relative to their peers. Regardless of social background, an average student would increase from about the 30th percentile to about the 60th percentile as a result of experiencing high versus low authentic pedagogy.

Box 5 gives examples of student performance from a high- and a low-pedagogy class.[13]

Box 5

STUDENT PERFORMANCE FROM HIGH AND LOW AUTHENTIC PEDAGOGY CLASSES

High Authentic Pedagogy

At the beginning of Ms. R's fifth- and sixth-grade social studies classes (usually 90 minutes in length), students often read silently for ten or fifteen minutes. The silent reading was usually followed up at a later time with group discussions and written reports or projects that Ms. R displayed in the classroom. Ms. R tried to keep the students thinking, prodding them, as the CORS observer noted, "to be creative, to 'stretch' themselves further."

During a class on the Netsilik people, Ms. R used a series of questions to orchestrate a discussion—Why were the Netsilik called the seal people? What have you learned about plants in the tundra? Why would the Netsilik be so dependent on seals? Why did the Netsilik place a higher priority on men than on women? All the questions involved students in interpretation of and generalization from data; adequate answers could not be gleaned simply from recall of the text.

Ms. R had her class of fifth- and sixth-graders research and write a paper on ecology. This assignment occupied 40 hours of class time during the 12-week grading period. Each student produced several drafts of the paper and met individually with the teacher several times to discuss the drafts. Students also received 11 pages of written directions on how to research, organize, and write the paper, including a step-by-step checklist for completing the assignment, a sample outline, and sample bibliography entries. The paper counted for 75 percent of the grade for the 12-week period.

The student whose work is excerpted here submitted seven pages of text, including an introduction to the topic she chose—sea turtles—an overview of issues to be discussed in the paper, detailed information on sea turtle biology drawn from several sources, and information on hazards faced by sea turtles in Costa Rica. Another section entitled "What you can do to help" included a phone number to call for more information, and advice on how to write the U.S. government to push for more protection of turtles. The student's work scored a 10 on our scale of 3 to 12.

The sea turtles are killed for meat and leather, their eggs are taken for food. Their nesting sites are destroyed by man, so they can develop buildings and other places to visit. On some of the beaches they offer boat rides. The boats are located on the sand when they are not being used. The owners are not aware that the boats are resting on top of the sea turtle eggs and killing them.

The sea turtles are classified under two families. The Leatherback and the Regular Sea turtles. The Leatherback Sea Turtles are the largest of the two.

There are alot of unanswered questions today relating to the sea turtles. Despite the explosion of sea turtle research, scientist are frustrated. One of the scientist was quoted saying "I don't know any branch of science where we have applied so much effort and learned so little". "We don't know where each species grows to maturity, or how long it takes them to grow up, or what the survival rates are".

Some of the answers can now be researched because the U.S. and 115 other countries have banned import or export of sea turtle products. By spreading the word and joining support groups, we can also slow down the process.

We can all help by keeping the beaches free of trash and pollution. We can make suggestions to the beach control unit to keep pleasure boating down and only allow it in certain areas where hatching does not take place. Sea turtles have a one percent chance of living to maturity, unlike you and I. We have a greater chance of living a very long life.

Box 5 (continued)

Low Authentic Pedagogy

During the four times CORS researchers observed Ms. A's fifth-grade hour-long social studies class, students read aloud from the textbook—a routine occasionally punctuated with Ms. A's asking factual recall questions. During one of the classes, students copied a chart from the board that organized the facts from the reading into categories. After finding more facts to fill up the chart, the students then completed a worksheet crossword puzzle built from the vocabulary words of the lesson. Rarely engaging the class in substantive conversation, Ms. A praised quiet and orderly behavior.

Ms. A assigned an assessment task that required students to copy a set of questions about famous explorers from a work sheet and to add the correct short-answer responses in the appropriate spots. The class spent 30 minutes on this exercise, which was part of a larger unit on exploration, and which Ms. A described as "very consistent" with what is typical in the class.

Ms. A scored 13.5 on our authentic pedagogy scale, which ranges from a low of 11 to a high of 43. Even though the student whose work is represented here did almost all the work correctly, the work scored 3.5 on our authentic achievement scale (which ranges from a low of 3 to a high of 12), because it demonstrated virtually no analysis or conceptual understanding.

99/A Super!

1. Prince Henry encouraged navigation.
2. An important instrument for sea captains was a compass.
3. After Columbus there were many Europeans expeditions to explore the Americas.
4. The Aztec and Inca civilizations were destroyed by conquistadors.
5. A legend helped Cortes conquer the Aztecs.
6. After Columbus, Europeans started coming to the Americas to live in colonies.
7. Europeans who came to the new world included missionaries.
8. Several explorers searched for a northwest passage.

NELS:88 Results

The NELS high schools varied in the degree of restructuring they reported. About 46 percent were classified as having at least three significant restructuring practices in place in 1990; another 43 percent had several traditional reform practices in place; and 11 percent had no reform practices in place.[14] CORS-sponsored studies have found that restructuring high schools, compared to those with only traditional practices or no reform practices, showed more impressive achievement gains in mathematics, reading, history, and science from grades 8 to 10 and also from grades 10 to 12.[15]

Another recent NELS study called special attention to achievement in mathematics and science and found that restructuring high schools had higher levels of authentic instruction in these subjects than either traditional reforming or nonreforming high schools.[16] Students in schools with higher levels of authentic instruction had higher achievement gains. Figure 3 shows the effects of these school differences from grades 8 to 10 and 10 to 12 in both mathematics and science.[17] In both subjects, both early and late in high school, achievement gains were substantially larger in schools with higher levels of authentic instruction. The increment in gain points between the low and high instruction schools ranged from about 50 percent to 100 percent. For example, an average student who attended a "high authentic instruction" school would learn about 78 percent more mathematics between grades 8 and 10 than a comparable student in a "low authentic instruction" school.

The NELS findings tell us that students who attend restructuring high schools learn more on conventional tests of achievement than those in more traditional schools, that restructuring high schools tend to have higher levels of authentic instruction, and that authentic instruction has a big effect on the differences in achievement gains between schools.

Equity

SRS and NELS also yielded encouraging findings on equity: Both studies showed that restructuring can help equalize students' opportunities to learn. The SRS showed that authentic pedagogy brings equal achievement benefits to students of different gender, socioeconomic status, race, and ethnicity. NELS showed that restructuring can even reduce inequalities in achievement between students of high and low socioeconomic status.

In the SRS study of highly restructured schools, we found that classrooms differed considerably in their levels of authentic pedagogy, but this variation was not related to students' gender, socioeconomic status, race, or ethnicity.[18] The NELS study also found considerable variability in authentic instruction within schools, but some schools were able to maintain both high levels and low

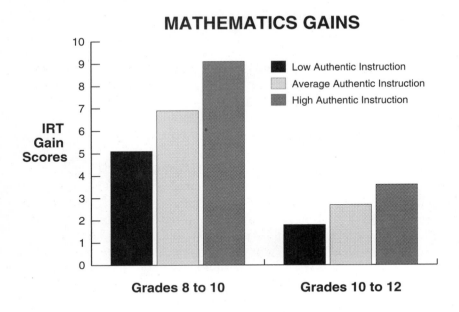

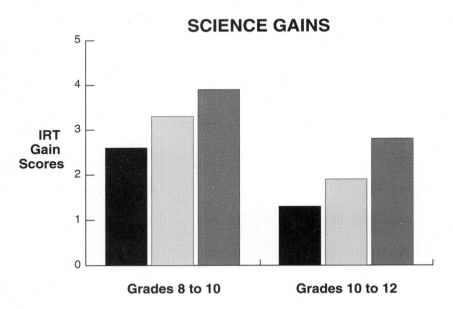

Figure 3: Mathematics and Science Achievement Gains in High Schools with Low, Average, and High Levels of Authentic Instructional Practices. (See Note 17.)

variability in authentic instruction. In other words, it is possible to deliver authentic instruction so that students from all social backgrounds have equal opportunity to learn.

More importantly, equal access to authentic pedagogy pays off in a more equitable distribution of achievement. Using analytical techniques that controlled for effects of students' social background, both the SRS and NELS studies showed that authentic pedagogy contributes to learning for all students.

Even so, it is possible that authentic pedagogy might serve some students better than others. In the SRS, we asked whether the achievement benefits of authentic pedagogy depended on students' social background. We found that the level of authentic pedagogy in a class exerted the same effects on student performance, regardless of gender, SES, race, and ethnicity.[19] The NELS studies found that the relationship between achievement gain and socioeconomic status was lower in restructuring high schools, compared to those with traditional or no reforms. The relationship between socioeconomic status and achievement gain also was lower in schools that had a more equal distribution of authentic instruction among their students.[20]

Having found that authentic pedagogy enhances student achievement, that it can be delivered equitably, and that it contributes to more equitable distribution of achievement, we now ask: "How can schools build the organizational capacity to promote authentic pedagogy? Section III explains how schools organized as professional communities are more likely to be effective in developing an intellectual focus for student learning and authentic pedagogy to sustain it.

III.
ORGANIZATIONAL CAPACITY: SCHOOLS AS PROFESSIONAL COMMUNITIES

Limits of Restructuring

We have seen that school restructuring can promote authentic teaching that helps to boost student achievement for all students. But this good news must be qualified: the tools of school restructuring do not assure a schoolwide focus on learning of high intellectual quality or authentic teaching. In fact, we found several schools in which restructuring activities did not advance the intellectual quality of student learning.

Why? First, teachers, parents, and students were seriously occupied with other tasks and goals for schooling. To develop students' intellect, schools must provide a safe and orderly environment, and they must socialize students to behave as responsible members of the school. In addition, schools are expected to instill democratic values, to contribute to students' physical and emotional health, to offer engaging extracurricular activities, to provide adult supervision when parents are not available, and to facilitate student placement into jobs and further schooling. In some schools, teachers and administrators spent a good deal of time and energy trying to maintain an orderly environment conducive to learning and trying to achieve the other legitimate goals of school. Sometimes, preoccupation with these activities deflected attention from the quality of learning. As staff became involved with issues of student conduct, with supervision of extracurricular activity, with administrative and managerial tasks such as taking attendance or keeping records, and with students' and parents' emotional concerns, intellectual priorities could slip into the background.

We also found that restructuring initiatives themselves generated a host of new issues that could divert staff attention from the agenda for learning. For example, adoption of techniques such as cooperative learning groups, use of portfolios, or student independent research projects raised a number of issues about how to manage and supervise students. Adoption of shared governance and team planning expanded the potential for interpersonal conflict and power struggles. When significant reforms were implemented without full faculty support, sometimes reformers understandably became more preoccupied with how to generate support within the school than with the intellectual quality of teacher and student work.

To be sure, we also found examples of innovative structures being used to accentuate attention to student learning of high quality. In these schools, teacher teams offered important support for their peers in crafting more intellectually rigorous and engaging curriculum. Longer class periods afforded important time for students to study topics in greater depth. Small group, cooperative learning activities provided useful venues for students to participate in substantive conversation. In short, the challenge is not just to adopt innovation, but to learn how to use new structures to enhance faculty and student concern for learning of high intellectual quality. Without aiming toward this end, there is little reason to implement innovative structures.

Why were some schools more successful than others in using the tools of restructuring to enhance the intellectual quality of students' work? The answer lies largely in the idea of organizational capacity.

Organizational Capacity

A school's success in educating students depends on the commitment and competence of individuals within the staff. Some prominent education reform efforts are aimed, therefore, at recruiting, training, or licensing competent individual professionals. But as in businesses, social service agencies, military units, or churches, schools have organizational norms, activities, and structures that greatly influence school productivity. Previous research shows that student achievement gains and other benefits are influenced by organizational characteristics beyond the skills of individual staff.[21]

High level professional skills are obviously critical. But we saw schools with competent teachers that lacked the organizational capacity to be effective with many students. When schools are unable to coordinate teachers' diverse aims for students into a curricular mission focused on high quality student learning, when teachers have few opportunities to work together to devise approaches suited to the school's student body, or when schools pursue multiple innovations without sustained, long-term consistency, it is difficult for even the most gifted teachers to make a positive difference for students.

The task for schools, then, is not simply to offer space and opportunity for individual teachers to teach. It is to organize human, technical, and social resources into an effective collective enterprise. This challenge may be taken for granted or overlooked, but it is an important cultural resource for the school, because it too is necessary for student learning.

What, beyond competent individuals, does a school need to create high organizational capacity? First, schools must find ways to generate clarity and consensus about central goals for student learning. These goals should be specific enough to sustain a coherent focus over time and to encourage further development of the mission. The school must then build collective responsibility among staff and students to cooperate, collaborate, and work for the mission.

In schools that CORS researchers considered successful, the mission for learning was powerful enough to guide instruction, but also flexible enough to encourage debate, discussion, and experimentation within the framework. These schools supported continuous reflection aimed at individual and organizational growth. They accomplished this in part by enhancing teacher access to knowledge and ideas beyond the school. Through deliberate promotion of professional development opportunities, the more successful schools further strengthened both the commitment and competence of individual staff members and the collective learning of the staff as a whole.

To achieve consensus on learning goals and professional growth, the school and staff within it must have the authority to act. The school needs the discretionary authority to act according to the staff's best professional judgment, with minimum interference from bureaucratic directives or political pressure that can undermine, rather than promote, the intellectual quality of student learning.

Professional Community and Why It Helps

Organizational capacity is enhanced when schools are shaped into professional communities. Just as authentic achievement provides a vision to inspire student learning of high intellectual quality, an image of the school as a professional community can help cultivate organizational capacity.

Professional community has connotations relevant to many different fields, such as law, medicine, or journalism, but as applied to schools, we think it is best described by three general features:

- Teachers pursue a clear shared purpose for all students' learning.

- Teachers engage in collaborative activity to achieve the purpose.

- Teachers take collective responsibility for student learning.

We found that professional community improves student learning. But before presenting the results, we explain why these features seem critical to effective teaching and student learning.

First, when students and teachers send clear and consistent messages to one another about the objectives and methods of learning, learning is more likely, because student and faculty effort can be directed more effectively toward intellectual ends. When school goals are vague or when consensus is low, teachers may feel comfortable with the autonomy they have to pursue their unique interests. But individual autonomy can reduce teacher efficacy when teachers can't count on colleagues to reinforce their objectives. In contrast, clear shared goals maximize teacher success through collective reinforcement.

Second, collaborative activity can enhance teachers' technical competence. As teachers work with students from increasingly diverse social backgrounds, and as the curriculum begins to demand more intellectual rigor, teachers require information, technical expertise, and social-emotional support far beyond the resources they can muster as individuals working alone. When teachers collaborate productively, they participate in reflective dialogue to learn more about professional issues; they observe and react to one another's teaching, curriculum, and assessment practices; and they engage in joint planning and curriculum development. By enriching teachers' technical and social resources, collaboration can make teaching more effective.

Third, clearly shared purpose and collaboration contribute to collective responsibility: one's colleagues share responsibility for the quality of all students' achievement. This norm helps to sustain each teacher's commitment. A culture of collective responsibility puts more peer pressure and accountability on staff who may not have carried their fair share, but it can also ease the burden on teachers who have worked hard in isolation but who felt unable to help some students. In short, professional community within the teaching staff sharpens the educational focus and enhances the technical and social support that teachers need to be successful.

Student learning depends ultimately on student effort, and to put forth the effort that ambitious learning requires, students need to be pushed. School competes for students' attention, which otherwise turns to personal problems and crises, jobs, taking care of family or friends, extracurricular activities, and popular culture's preoccupation with videos, the latest CDs, cars, clothes, and other commercial trappings. If teachers and parents leave it up to students to choose whether or not to learn, many students will be left behind. Instead, adults must take active responsibility for student success. Strong teacher professional community provides a consistently demanding and supportive environment that pushes students to do their best.

As a result of strong professional community, students learn that:

- They are expected to work hard to master challenging academic material.

•Staff and peers have confidence that, in the long run, students will be successful if they work hard on academic tasks.

•Staff will give them help and support, both through individual teaching/tutoring and by establishing classroom norms where learning is taken seriously, where peers are expected to help one another, and where students have the opportunity to make mistakes and to try again without being judged "stupid."

Together, these expectations and behaviors establish a climate where students take learning seriously and help one another to succeed. Professional community generates the critical social support that students need for ambitious learning. The more successful schools we studied were able to use tools of restructuring to strengthen professional community.

Professional Community Enhances Student Achievement

We found that the level of professional community in a school had significant effects on student achievement whether achievement was measured as authentic performance or tested in more conventional ways. The effects of professional community on authentic performance in mathematics and social studies are evident in two main results from the School Restructuring Study (SRS) of 24 elementary, middle, and high schools:[22]

• Schoolwide teacher professional community affected the level of classroom authentic pedagogy, which in turn affected student performance.

• Schoolwide teacher professional community affected the level of social support for student learning, which in turn affected student performance.[23]

Figure 4 shows the impact of these combined findings. Overall, if we compared two "average" students, one in a school with low teacher professional community, and the other in a school with high professional community, the students in a high community school would score about 27 percent higher on the SRS measure. This difference would represent a gain of 31 percentile points.[24]

Confidence in these findings from the highly selective sample of SRS schools increases when we consider results from the NELS national sample of about 800 high schools. The NELS study included a far broader range of schools and showed the effects of professional community on student achievement when tested through more conventional multiple choice items.[25]

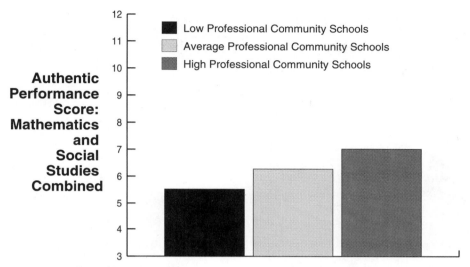

Figure 4: Levels of Authentic Student Performance for Students in Schools with Low, Average, and High Professional Community in Restructuring Elementary, Middle, and High Schools. (See Note 24.)

Among the key findings:

- We considered high levels of academic course taking, along with low variability of such course taking within a school, an indicator that teachers and students were pursuing a common curriculum that reflected a shared purpose focused on high intellectual quality. In schools where students took more mathematics and science courses and where the variability in number of mathematics and science courses taken was lower, learning was greater.[26] Figure 5 shows the results.[27]

- In schools where teachers reported higher levels of collective responsibility for student learning, also a key criterion for professional community, learning was greater in mathematics, science, reading, and history. Figure 6 shows the results for mathematics and science.[28]

- In schools where students were pressed toward academic pursuits and expected to do homework, and where students placed high priority on learning, performance was greater in science. We considered this measure of academic press an indicator of social support for learning as described above. Figure 7 shows the results.[29]

MATHEMATICS GAINS

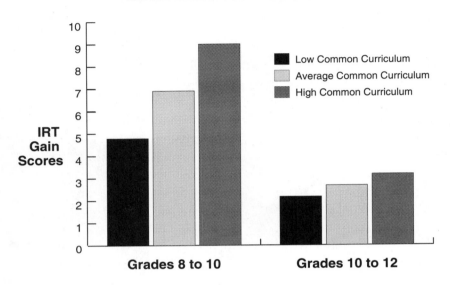

SCIENCE GAINS

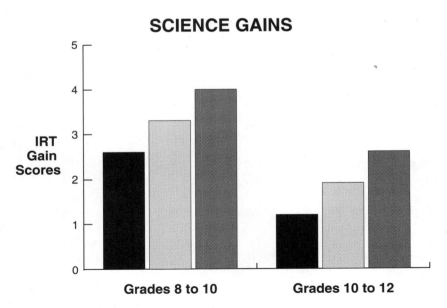

Figure 5: Mathematics and Science Achievement Gains in High Schools with Low, Average, and High Levels of Common Curriculum. (See Notes 17 and 27.)

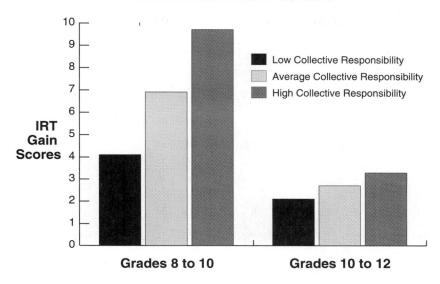

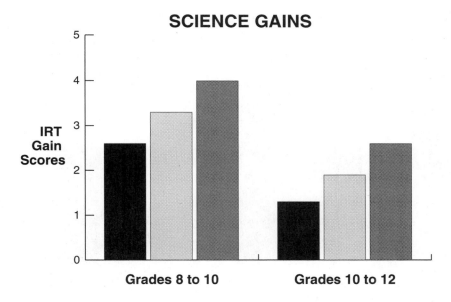

Figure 6: Mathematics and Science Achievement Gains in High Schools with Low, Average, and High Levels of Collective Responsibility. (See Notes 17 and 28.)

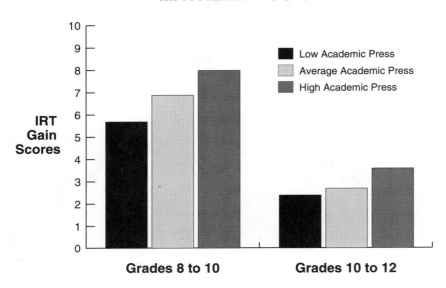

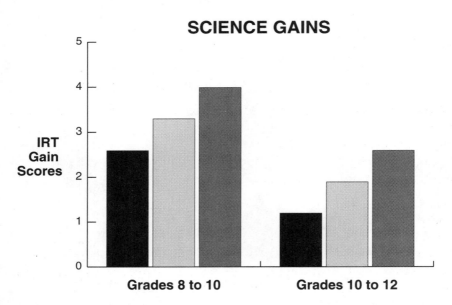

Figure 7: Mathematics and Science Achievement Gains in High Schools with Low, Average, and High Levels of Academic Press. (See Notes 17 and 29.)

In reviewing results of Figures 5-7, and considering mathematics and science gains between grades 8 to 10 and 10 to 12, we found that students in schools scoring high on the three indicators would have the following achievement gains over students in schools scoring low:[30]

Common Curriculum—from 46 percent to 100 percent higher.

Collective Responsibility—from 54 percent to 137 percent higher.

Academic Press—from 38 percent to 60 percent higher.

For example, Figure 6 shows that a student in a high collective responsibility school would learn more than twice as much science between grades 10 and 12; that is, the gain would be 116 percent of the gain of a comparable student in the low collective responsibility school.

High levels of academic course taking, collective responsibility for students' learning, and academic press also reduced the traditionally strong relationship between socioeconomic status and achievement gains in mathematics and science. In this sense, professional community not only boosted student achievement gains, it also helped to make the gains more equitable among socioeconomic groups.

The main implication of these findings from the SRS and NELS studies is that, if schools want to enhance their organizational capacity to boost student learning, they should work on building professional community that is characterized by shared purpose, collaborative activity, and collective responsibility among school staff.

Conditions That Support Professional Community

How can schools become professional communities? The challenge is to assemble and cultivate a staff with the technical competence and commitment to work productively as a group for the intellectual accomplishment of all students. Success depends largely upon human resources and leadership, but structural conditions can also help.

Human Resources and Leadership

The effectiveness of a school staff depends much on the quality of school leadership and the available pool of talent in the existing teacher population. Effective school leaders—especially principals, but also teacher leaders—can make a big difference through hiring, staff development, and establishing a supportive school climate. We encountered principals who consistently emphasized a clear intellectual mission for the school, who hired staff to teach toward the mission, and who found ways to transfer dissident or less competent teachers. Some principals stimulated professional discussion by circulating books and articles about research and stimulating ideas and by supporting continuous staff development on topics such as assessment, writing, and interdisciplinary curriculum.

In schools with stronger professional communities, we found that principals and staff enhanced their resources by reinforcing a climate of support and respect for teachers' work and by pursuing a continuous cycle of innovation, feedback, and redesign in curriculum, instruction, and assessment.

Structural Conditions

Certain structural conditions can also strengthen professional community. We found three important facilitating conditions: an interdependent work structure such as teaming, small size, and school-based authority for the operation of the school.

Interdependent work structure. When teachers work in groups that require coordination, this, by definition, involves collaboration. When groups, rather than individuals, are seen as the main units for implementing curriculum, instruction, and assessment, they facilitate development of shared purposes for student learning and collective responsibility to achieve it.

The mere existence of a formal interdependent structure, however, is not enough. There must be time for the teams or other groups to communicate and work together. We saw examples of teachers being organized into teams, committees, or departments but having no significant periods of time to work together. In the SRS, professional community was higher in schools that had more time for planning in smaller groups, such as teams and committees with major responsibilities for instruction, curriculum, and assessment.[31] And in the NELS study of high schools, we found that schools with teams and higher levels of cooperation among faculty showed higher levels of collective responsibility.[32]

Small school size. We know from experience that it is easier to communicate and coordinate with others and to build trust, shared purpose, and collective responsibility for the welfare of the group when the group is smaller. This common-sense evidence that smaller schools facilitate professional community is supported by our research.

In the 24 elementary, middle, and high schools of the SRS, higher professional community occurred in schools ranging in enrollment from 385 to 1,000 and rarely occurred in schools beyond 1,200.[33] A study of 210 Chicago elementary schools showed that the level of professional community was higher in schools of 350 students or less.[34]

Both studies, however, found examples of smaller schools with low levels of professional community and larger schools with strong professional communities. This finding suggests that, like other structural features, small size is a facilitating condition for strong professional community, but not a sufficient one.

There might be some range of school sizes that generally work better than others, and optimum range might depend upon the level. For example, the Chicago study found that the level of professional community in elementary schools with enrollments between 350 and 700 was much lower than the level for schools under 350, and was similar to the professional environment of elementary schools with more than 700 students. Similar research has not been completed for middle and high schools. Although we cannot specify an ideal range, our qualitative and quantitative findings clearly indicate that smaller school size facilities the building of professional community.[35]

School authority to act. The authority to implement a clear intellectual mission for student learning is a central requirement for school organizational capacity. In contrast, when school action is substantially constrained by external regulations, it becomes difficult for staff to feel a sense of ownership and collective responsibility for the school's success. Following rules and complying with mandates from superiors can become more important than doing whatever is necessary to help students learn.

School authority to act has two parts: the autonomy of the school from external constraints, and teachers' influence over their work within the school. Many of the schools we studied had significant authority over curriculum, school policies, and hiring, and some had substantial authority over budget as well. The schools most successful in building professional community had high levels of authority to act, both in terms of school autonomy and teacher influence.[36]

But the SRS and the study of school decentralization in Chicago also showed that school autonomy from external constraints offered no guarantee of high organizational capacity. In Chicago, for example, all schools began to operate with significant autonomy by around Fall 1990, but by 1993 not more than 40 percent had clearly embarked on significant reform programs, and about 25 percent experienced virtually no change.[37] In other words, school autonomy from external constraints may well be a necessary condition for school professional community, but it is certainly not sufficient. This issue is discussed further in Section IV.

In addition to autonomy from unreasonable constraints, staff within a school must have meaningful opportunities to influence the school's program and policy. Structures for shared decision-making can help, but again they are not sufficient. All Chicago schools and most of the SRS schools had structures for shared decision-making, but in many schools the principal maintained a level of control that sometimes stifled meaningful influence by teachers and parents. Regardless of a school's formal governance structure, teachers' control over their practice and over school policy contributed to professional community—in both the SRS and the national set of high schools in the NELS study.[38]

Like other structural conditions, school authority to act and opportunities for shared governance within a school enhanced professional community only when the school staff seized the opportunity to use this authority in constructive ways. In the next section of this report, we show that support from external agencies, especially through standard setting and staff development, can help the school use its authority more productively.

In short, we found that effective schools have more than competent individual staff: They have the organizational capacity to work productively as a group for high quality learning for all students. Schools that operate as strong professional communities contribute to student achievement and to equitable distribution of achievement, whether measured in "authentic" or conventional ways. Structural conditions can be helpful in building schoolwide professional community, but they alone cannot assure success without a solid base of human resources and leadership. These resources can be enhanced through external support, which is described next.

IV.
EXTERNAL SUPPORT FOR STUDENT LEARNING AND ORGANIZATIONAL CAPACITY

T o build the organizational capacity required to promote student learning of high intellectual quality, schools need support from beyond their walls. We found a wide variety of external agents attempting to help schools to restructure. They included state legislatures, district administrations, universities, unions, professional organizations, foundations, courts, parents, and the federal government.

In the schools we studied, districts, states, parents, and private nonprofit organizations working for educational reform—we call them independent developers—were the most active and influential. These external agents helped schools to increase intellectual quality and organizational capacity through four strategies: standard setting, staff development, deregulation, and support from parents.[39]

External Standard Setting

H igh standards for student learning are central to successful school restructuring. Without clear, high standards for learning, school restructuring is like a rudderless ship. Where can schools find help in developing a vision based on high intellectual standards? Teachers, administrators, and parents all brought ideas and knowledge to bear on this question. However, the validation of standards generated at a school ultimately depends on their acceptance by professional and civic constituencies beyond the individual school.

We found educators considering a number of sources for standards. For example, teachers reported being influenced by books and reports from professional organizations, such as the National Council of Teachers of Mathematics (NCTM), and by independent developers, such as the Coalition of Essential Schools and the Accelerated Schools initiative. Some states had mandated standards for public schools. Whether mandated or voluntary, the array of external influences stimulated professional dialogue and prompted some attempts within schools to define and implement high standards for student performance and school accountability.

Because of the political authority vested in states, their standard setting initiatives attracted more serious attention than voluntary initiatives. States promoted standard setting through traditional competency and achievement testing and also through new forms of assessment and curriculum frameworks. State testing programs we observed included New York's Regents Competency Test (RCT), the Texas Assessment of Academic Skills (TAAS), and the California Test of Basic Skills (CTBS). Standards reflecting more authentic assessment were found in the now defunct California Learning Assessment System (CLAS), the Kentucky Instructional Results Information System (KIRIS), and the Vermont Assessment Program.

Since state-sponsored forms of authentic assessment were relatively new, they had yet to produce broad impact on instruction or on student achievement. But many of these mandates conveyed high expectations for improving student learning. Some politicians and members of the public were impatient in expecting the new assessments to produce both reliable indicators of, and clear improvements in, student achievement. While California, Vermont, and Kentucky each experienced political and/or technical problems with their assessment efforts, they succeeded in stimulating broad discussion of the importance of high standards as the basis for school reform.

Although only recently implemented, the Kentucky Education Reform Act (KERA) had some potential to elevate intellectual quality in schools, because its assessment system called for students to use complex academic knowledge and skills. For example, at the high school level students were assessed through three strategies: problem solving using state-developed paper-and-pencil tests, portfolios in mathematics and writing, and state administered "performance events" that emphasized applying knowledge and the solving of real-world problems in group settings. Generally, teachers viewed state testing with skepticism, but they also tended to endorse efforts like those in Kentucky, which promised to improve conventional competency and achievement testing by making it more authentic.

Independent developers such as the Coalition of Essential Schools, the Accelerated Schools initiative, and the New Standards Project also played a role in helping schools to emphasize and clarify intellectual standards for student work. But in most cases that we observed, these projects had only nascent influence. A salient example of standard setting by a professional organization was NCTM's standards for mathematics; these were influential in a number of schools we studied. Discussion of NCTM standards elevated mathematics teachers' knowledge of their field, but because they were specific to mathematics, these particular standards could not serve as a schoolwide framework for intellectual quality.

Adopting standards issued by professional organizations and independent developers was a voluntary option for schools. Not surprisingly, those schools that made the best use of such standards were already inclined to see the need for them. In general, these schools contained a high level of human resources; i.e., staff were motivated to search for help and to draw ideas and insights from external resources about standards and how to put them into practice.

Staff Development

S taff development from districts, universities, and professional developers provided another form of support for restructuring. These agents offered help on topics such as shared decision making, cooperative learning, reading instruction, and assessment by portfolio. For example, 15 of the 24 schools in the School Restructuring Study (SRS) had staff development sessions on the use of portfolios or some other aspect of authentic assessment. In many cases, however, only a small portion of a school's staff participated in these opportunities. Individual teacher choice to participate in staff development was typical in many schools. Some staff often became excited about an idea or practice, but frequently many of their colleagues remained uninformed and unmoved. The result was fragmentation, rather than a consistent schoolwide effort.

In contrast to staff development that was limited, fragmented, or episodic, we found some examples of entire staffs immersed in continuous and coordinated programs. In such cases, the impact was schoolwide and much more powerful. The following example describes such a program.

Careen Elementary was opened as a new school by a large urban district to demonstrate and further develop what they called Applied Learning. The approach grew out of dissatisfaction in the district, and in the local business community, with the quality of public school graduates. In response, the school board and superintendent initiated a program focused on the application of academic skills and knowledge to real-world problems and settings. The district established Careen Elementary to test the potential value of Applied Learning. If the school proved successful, its curriculum and instructional practices would be replicated and diffused throughout the district.

Careen was a school of choice for both students and staff. A lottery insured that the student population of about 385 would reflect the diversity of Anglo, Hispanic, and African-American students in the district. A central office administrator recruited for the school a select group of experienced teachers judged to be highly skilled and also sympathetic to the premises of Applied Learning. Careen offered teachers a stimulating educational environment on the cutting edge of their profession.

The district obtained a sizeable grant from a local foundation to provide continuous staff development on Applied Learning for the Careen staff. The grant included stipends for teachers to attend a series of Saturday sessions during the academic year, plus summer workshops. Participation was required.

In these sessions, teachers read from a diverse set of authors from John Dewey to Grant Wiggins. Topics focused mainly on issues of curriculum and assessment. Some activities were unconventional: For example, during one summer workshop, teachers visited local businesses to study how mathematics and language skills were used in the world of work. During these sessions Careen staff began to translate the general principles of Applied Learning into a more specific curricular vision for the school.

The Applied Learning vision stressed that education should connect children's classroom experiences to the demands of adult society, and that students should be responsible for conceiving and carrying out important work. Using ideas and material from staff development sessions, teachers planned, tried, and evaluated a number of ideas. For example, a first-grade class decided to create a museum with dioramas and artifacts to depict the state's diverse ecologies. The project required the children to conduct research and contact a number of experts outside the school to obtain artifacts. Fourth-graders in this school launched a newspaper with the help of local professional journalists, who became mentors to the project. When the school needed new playground equipment, students did research on the costs, safety factors, and appeal of various playground paraphernalia.

If students needed to go on a field trip as part of a project, the school had to obtain permission from the district. Consistent with Applied Learning's effort to prepare young people for the kind of thinking and activity needed for success in life outside of school, students crafted a letter to the appropriate administrator, stating an educational purpose for the trip, indicating how it would be supervised, and so on. Similarly, if a class wanted to know more about the ecological function of wetlands, they wrote a letter to the Nature Conservancy to obtain information or seek a speaker for class.

Staff development challenged teachers to invent ways of teaching that were consistent with the school's vision of student performance. For example, staff development supported teachers' work on portfolios as a vehicle for demonstrating student achievement, and in lieu of graded report cards teachers wrote extended narratives for parents describing what each student could do with his or her knowledge.

Behind the scenes, a key district administrator worked tirelessly to make the school a success. Resourceful in generating financial and human resources to support the program, she pushed hard for a sustained staff development program. The program helped the Careen staff begin the task of creating a set of standards and practices that most local educators and parents judged successful.

Deregulation: Autonomy and Authority to Act

Earlier we explained that a school's authority to act on vital matters was essential to building organizational capacity in general and professional community in particular. Schools that showed serious concern for high quality student learning also had considerable autonomy to define their mission and to carry it out. To illustrate how state and district deregulation helped a school to focus on intellectual quality and professional community, we describe Okanagon Middle School, one of two charter schools we studied.

Located in the Far West, Okanagon was created when the district gave a principal and a core group of teachers the authority to plan and implement a mission for a new neighborhood school. Okanagon served 1,350 mostly poor and minority students: 34 percent African American, 17 percent Hispanic, 8 percent Anglo, and 41 percent Asian. Fifty-four percent qualified for free or reduced-price lunch.

The staff secured grants from the state and from foundations to support planning, development, and implementation of school restructuring. With these funds, the staff held retreats, visited other restructuring schools, purchased books on school reform, and met to discuss ideas about the kind of school that would best serve the poor and minority children from the school's neighborhood. External support made possible a rich dialogue that forged consensus around the intellectual goals of the school and the kinds of practices that would promote them.

In fact, the state grant required Okanagon's staff to address the issue of intellectual goals. Staff developed formal written academic standards to guide students' and teachers' work. They also created a set of campus and classroom behavior standards for students. These two sets of explicit standards shaped the day-to-day language and expectations of students, parents, and staff who saw the standards as important guides to teaching, learning, and personal behavior.

Although the district had granted the staff considerable authority to invent a new school, eventually they found that some district regulations still interfered with their work. Consequently, when a new state law offered the possibility of increased autonomy through charter status, Okanagon staff voted to pursue it. Charter status protected the school from sudden changes in local political conditions because, by law, a charter waived almost all state and district regulations affecting an individual school. The charter application process also required staff to further clarify the path of development reflected in the philosophy and practices they had already implemented.

With the granting of the charter, Okanagon was assured the authority to make decisions in several areas crucial to carrying out its vision. Most important from the staff's point of view was the freedom to select staff who embraced the school's vision without being restricted by seniority rights stipulated in the district-union negotiated agreement. The school used its authority to eliminate counselors from the staff, because the school's vision called for teachers to undertake an extended role that included counseling.

The school also had the authority to pursue ground-breaking collaboration with a number of public and private human service organizations to better serve the social and health needs of its students. To coordinate services from multiple social agencies, the school and the county created a new organization that operated independently of the district. The new organization was able to blend different funding streams for student support services, something that had previously proved difficult for schools to accomplish.

Okanagon was typical of a number of schools in the SRS that sought autonomy to act on a mission aimed at high quality learning. But charter status was only one route to such autonomy. Other schools obtained it through district and state waivers or by becoming officially recognized within a special category of alternative or experimental schools. Such schools were given authority to march to a different drummer, one that they had chosen and believed in. For those with a clear mission for learning and the commitment to pursue it, district deregulation was a decisive form of external support.

Autonomy: Not Always Enough

Chicago is the site of the country's most radical experiment in decentralization and deregulation of public schools. The rationale for decentralization is that schools will be more effective when professionals and parents familiar with students' needs make decisions on programs, staffing, and allocation of funds. State law requires that each Chicago school be governed by an elected Local School Council (LSC) composed of six parents, two community members, two teachers, and the principal. The principal serves at the discretion of the LSC, although teachers retain traditional tenure rights. The LSC has significant control over the school's budget, including a substantial amount of discretionary money from state categorical funds, which flows directly to the school based on student enrollment. Schools have the authority to use their funds to purchase help from external agencies, and some have developed extensive contacts with organizations to assist with restructuring and reform.[40] But as shown below, the authority to direct one's own reform is not necessarily a sufficient formula for success.

The Center for School Improvement (CSI) at the University of Chicago developed a partnership with several elementary schools to help them navigate the uncharted waters of decentralization and deregulation. One of these was Alexander, a K-8 school serving poor African Americans from a community that was "truly disadvantaged." Alexander's principal had restored order to a chaotic school several years earlier. Even with the election of an LSC, Alexander remained firmly and willingly under the principal's control. She was popular with her staff and parents, who looked to her for guidance and considered her the school's "mother" as well as principal.[41]

Alexander chose to focus on improving literacy instruction. With the help of CSI, staff development provided teachers with a framework and a set of practices to help students who had fallen behind. A literacy coordinator was chosen from the teaching staff to help teachers try out and implement new instructional strategies. At the end of the first year of intensive training and implementation, the teachers were very positive about the benefits of the new program. They also gave high praise to the literacy coordinator for the technical help and social support she provided.

However, as the next school year began, it became clear that the principal resented the accolades and professional status given the literacy coordinator. In both subtle and overt ways, the principal began to undermine the coordinator's authority by giving her additional administrative duties that interfered with implementing the literacy initiative. Efforts on behalf of the initiative declined as the coordinator was forced to spend more time on additional administrative duties assigned by the principal. CSI tried to continue support for the program, but the principal was unresponsive, even blocking some of its efforts.

Alexander illustrates how the social and political dynamics of local contexts can nullify the potential of deregulation. While local autonomy allowed Alexander to choose high quality professional assistance through CSI, internal politics undermined the initiative when the principal had difficulty accepting successful teacher leadership. Alexander functioned more like a dysfunctional family than a professional organization. The principal considered herself the "mother" of the school, and the family loyalty she engendered served to consolidate her power. While Alexander's LSC had the legal authority to replace the principal, it was either too passive or too trusting of her to make a change. The autonomy vested in the LSC was not used to promote a school reform agenda.

The SRS and Chicago studies revealed that those schools with a focus on student learning, strong human resources, and some capacity for a collective school effort could use autonomy productively. Such schools emphasized high quality learning, and they became stronger professional communities because autonomy freed them to act on their strengths. But for schools without a vision and the social resources to act collectively, autonomy through deregulation appeared relatively ineffective, at least in the short run.

Parent Involvement

Parents can exert powerful influences on schools, and many schools involved in restructuring worked hard to generate support from parents. While our research found many different ways for involving parents, participating in governance was strongly emphasized in a number of schools; parent involvement was seen as a way to build support for the school's mission. In the SRS, 14 of the 24 schools had some form of shared decision-making council that included parent membership. In Chicago, of course, all schools were run by LSCs, where parents comprised six of the eleven members. When governance was well conceived and implemented, parent participation tended to reinforce student learning and increase the school's organizational capacity. At one school, for example, parents helped to hire staff and raised substantial amounts of money to provide extra learning resources. Whether such participation succeeded in building support depended much upon the politics and leadership within a school.

For example, the Chicago study found that, even though all schools had the same governance structure, with parents holding majority power on every local school council, the quality of involvement varied considerably. A school's politics usually could be characterized as adversarial, consolidated principal power, or strong democratic. In schools characterized by adversarial politics, conflict between individuals and groups stymied progress toward building professional community. Principals who consolidated their power often inhibited professional community by preempting meaningful participation by teachers and parents. But strong democracy schools in Chicago usually encouraged discussion about the educational mission of the school, and even in the event of some conflict, schools with strong democracy promoted social trust and concern for the school's educational mission.[42]

The SRS also found that parent participation in governance took a variety of forms. Where the principal or staff had consolidated power, parent participation was largely symbolic; that is, although parents might appear at school meetings and even participate in voting, they actually exerted little influence on decisions, because professionals controlled the flow of information. In contrast, in a few schools information and power were broadly distributed to parents. In these schools, parents could become involved in substantive decision making that enhanced curriculum, instruction, and assessment. Examples of substantive involvement included parents conducting useful evaluations of curriculum, instruction, and assessment in the school, helping to hire a new principal, making budget decisions, raising money, and lobbying the school district to support the school's unique program.

In both the Chicago Study and the SRS, parent involvement contributed most to a school when it reflected consensus between parents and staff over the school's mission.[43] If there was general agreement about the school's mission, then parent involvement provided important help and reinforced collective responsibility for student success. Such consensus affirmed respect for the professionalism of the staff and promoted a strong effort on behalf of student learning.

On the other hand, significant conflict among parents, or between parents and the school, reduced the school's capacity for professional community. In Chicago, a small proportion of schools were stuck in adversarial politics, and the SRS observed divisive conflicts over policies about whole language versus phonics, the appropriateness of gifted and talented programs, and struggles among different parent groups in the selection of a principal.

In the long run, parent involvement initially born out of conflict could conceivably lead to a stronger school, and we saw evidence of this in at least one Chicago school.[44] But usually these conflicts tended to undermine professional community and the school's capacity to define a mission based on high quality learning.

Implications

We have shown how external agencies can help to enhance the intellectual quality of student learning and to build organizational capacity. But the examples also suggest that there is no clear set of approaches that all external agencies should adopt. If external support is to be effective, both schools and agencies should be aware of two important complexities.

First, none of the forms of external influence assure progress in student learning or organizational capacity. While professional organizations and states can promulgate standards for student achievement, their content can be trivial, or too vague, or learning outcomes too numerous to inspire high standards in schools. Staff development activities may focus only on techniques and procedures, rather than the quality of student work, and staff development may benefit only a few people, rather than building schoolwide capacity. Parents, meanwhile, can undermine as well as support a school's organizational capacity. Assuming that external agents promulgate high quality standards and provide useful staff development, implementing these well requires strong leadership and a receptive school culture, characteristics not present in all schools.

Second, external agencies differ in the power they have to influence schools. Compared to states or districts, independent developers, professional organizations, and parents have less legal or political authority. They also have fewer financial resources with which to offer significant long-term support. Independent developers, with less power to help schools, must limit their efforts to a relatively small proportion of schools, always relying on those schools that volunteer to participate . Districts and states have more legal, political, and economic power, but often bureaucratic tendencies limit their ability to deliver effective help to schools. Political compromise or conflict among competing interest groups, and continuing shifts in leadership at the state and district levels, often lead to confusion over strategies and long-term goals.

Again, the effectiveness of any strategy—standard setting, staff development, deregulation, or parent participation—depends substantially on the prior level of human and social resources in a school. Schools such as Careen and Okanagon benefitted from the staff development and autonomy provided by external agents because their staffs were ready to make good use of these opportunities. But a school such as Alexander, which received significant external assistance, could not make productive use of its opportunities. At Careen and Okanagon, effective leaders assembled committed staffs willing to work together for specific missions. At Alexander, however, conflicting loyalties within the school and problems in leadership reduced the school's capacity to make use of this kind of external support.

The SRS found that if a school was rich in human and social resources but did not already have autonomy, it struggled to obtain the authority to act on its self-developed vision. Securing such autonomy tended to strengthen intellectual quality and organizational capacity in that school. But schools that were poor in human and social resources had difficulty making good use of standards, staff development, parent support, or autonomy. It seemed that schools beginning with a low base of resources required more extensive and complex forms of support than were available from outside sources. Some judicious blend of standard setting, staff development, parent support, and deregulation would probably be appropriate for such schools, but we did not see impressive examples of external agencies blending the right mixture to successfully meet this challenge.[45]

V.
CONCLUSION

T he recent education reform movement gives too much attention to changes in school organization that do not directly address the quality of student learning. New administrative arrangements and teaching techniques contribute to improved learning only if they are carried out within a framework that focuses on learning of high intellectual quality. Such learning engages students in constructing knowledge, through disciplined inquiry, to produce discourse, products, and performances that have value beyond certifying success in school. Student learning can meet these high standards if educators and the public give students three kinds of support:

• Teachers who practice authentic pedagogy.

• Schools that build organizational capacity by strengthening professional community.

• External agencies and parents that support schools to achieve the high quality student learning we have described.

The CORS studies have shown that authentic pedagogy contributes equitably to student learning, whether measured according to standards for authentic performance or in more conventional ways. But practicing authentic pedagogy, especially throughout a school, is enormously difficult. Beyond training, or recruiting competent teachers, it calls for channeling individual human commitment and competence into collective organizational productivity. Schools need to have a clear, shared purpose for student learning, collaborative activity to achieve the purpose, and collective responsibility among teachers and students for student learning.

Attaining these conditions of professional community is a daunting task, but well worth the effort. We found that students in schools with higher levels of professional community learn more, whether learning is measured as authentic performance or in more conventional terms.

How can schools build professional community? The critical human norms and skills cannot be mechanically engineered by implementing new organizational structures. To the contrary, introducing structures and practices often has the opposite effect of diverting attention from the quality of student learning. The good news is that structural changes, when combined with certain human and social resources, can substantially strengthen school professional community, which elevates student learning.

The following structural conditions can enhance the professional community needed to promote learning of high intellectual quality:

- Shared governance that increases teachers' influence over school policy and practice.

- Interdependent work structures, such as teaching teams, which encourage collaboration.

- Staff development that enhances technical skills consistent with school missions for high quality learning.

- Deregulation that provides autonomy for schools to pursue a vision of high intellectual standards.

- Small school size, which increases opportunities for communication and trust.

- Parent involvement in a broad range of school affairs.

These conditions increase the success of educators and parents working together to enhance school organizational capacity to improve pedagogy and student learning. The most promising examples of strong organizational capacity aimed toward high intellectual standards were found in schools that began with a well-defined mission, the authority to hire staff consistent with the mission, and effective leaders who kept the school on track. Generally, these were schools of choice or schools with special status that freed them from conventional constraints. We found no examples where structural changes alone had transformed conventional schools into strong professional communities that met the Center's standards for high quality learning.

The findings suggest that practitioners and policymakers should concentrate first on the principles of intellectual quality, as represented in the vision of authentic achievement, and only secondarily on the specific structural tools of reform. External agencies need to encourage public dialogue about the importance of high quality student learning, with full recognition that this is a demanding long-term enterprise. Standard setting, staff development, and deregulation should be consistent with this purpose. In enlisting support from parents and community members, agencies and policymakers should expand public understanding of the meaning of, and need for, high quality learning.

In short, we know that students are capable of high quality performance and that teachers and schools can teach them to produce it. But to provide the necessary support for this work, districts, states, and independent reform agents must all keep their eye on the ball—student achievement of high intellectual quality.

NOTES

1. For reports of this study, see Berends and King (1994); Kruse, Louis, and Bryk (1994, Spring); Louis, Marks, and Kruse (1995); Lynn (1994); Newmann (1991); Newmann and Associates (in press); Newmann, Marks, and Gamoran (1995); Newmann, Secada, and Wehlage (1995); Peterson and Warren (1994).

2. For reports of this study, see Lee and Smith (1993, 1994, 1995, in press); Lee, Smith, and Croninger (1995).

3. For reports of this study, see Bryk, Easton, Kerbow, Rollow, and Sebring (1993, in preparation); Bryk, Easton, Rollow, and Sebring (1994); Bryk and Rollow (1992); Rollow, and Bryk (1995); Sebring et al. (1995).

4. For reports of this study, see Kruse (1994); Kruse and Louis (1995); Louis and King (1993); Louis, Kruse, and Associates (1995).

5. Teachers, administrators, parents, students, and others who participated in the Center's studies were promised confidentiality in order to protect them from public exposure that could put them at personal risk. All schools are, therefore, identified by pseudonyms.

6. A more elaborate version of the vision, standards, and scoring for authentic achievement is presented in Newmann, Secada, and Wehlage (1995). Material in Boxes 2-4 is taken from this source.

7. These standards represent only a limited view of the quality of classroom instruction, one focused on authentic intellectual quality. A broader, more complete look at instruction would also include features such as orderly classroom atmosphere, student cooperation, and coherence among daily lessons that connect to a larger unit of study.

High quality student performance on authentic tasks also demands consistent support for all students to master challenging work. The instructional climate should communicate high expectations for all and should cultivate, through both teacher and peer behavior, enough trust and respect to reward serious effort. Qualities of social support are necessary to nurture authentic achievement, but since they are not uniquely tied to the concept of authentic intellectual quality, they were not included in our standards. Social support for student achievement is emphasized in Section III.

8. Newmann, Secada, and Wehlage (1995) explain the standards in more detail and suggest how teachers can use them.

9. The standards presented here seem appropriate for the core academic subjects, but we have not applied them to subjects such as music, art, industrial arts, or physical education.

10. Instructional practice items in NELS offered approximations mainly for the standards of higher order thinking (e.g., how often students design experiments and make up scientific problems) and substantive conversation (e.g., how often students explain work orally and participate in student led group discussion). NELS items tapped aspects of teachers' instruction but did not include measures of authentic assessment practice.

11. Reports of this study are available in Newmann, Marks, and Gamoran (1995) and Marks, Newmann, and Gamoran (in press).

12. The analysis included 2,100 students in 125 classrooms in 23 schools. Most students had either a mathematics or social studies score, and the two subjects were scored on the same 12-point scale. There were no major differences in the effect of authentic pedagogy on achievement between the two subjects. Since student performance was scored according to expectations within each grade level, one would not necessarily expect the scores to increase from elementary to high school.

Levels of authentic pedagogy were defined as follows: low = authentic pedagogy 1 standard deviation (SD) below the mean for all SRS classes; average = mean level of authentic pedagogy for all SRS classes; high = authentic pedagogy 1 SD above the mean for all SRS classes. An "average" student was defined as one who scored at the mean (in the SRS sample) on self-reported socioeconomic status and on National Assessment of Educational Progress (NAEP) test items administered prior to the measures of authentic performance. Estimates are averaged across males and females and students of different racial and ethnic backgrounds. Estimates take into account the effects of gender, socioeconomic status, race/ethnicity, and NAEP score on authentic performance.

13. The material in Box 5 is taken from Marks, Newmann, and Gamoran (in press).

14. Examples of restructuring practices include students keeping the same homeroom throughout high school, interdisciplinary teaching teams, mixed ability classes in mathematics and science, school-within-a-school, parents volunteering in the school. Examples of traditional practices include departmentalization with chairs, common classes for the same curricular track, increased graduation requirements, parent-teacher conferences each semester, student evaluation of course content. See Lee and Smith (1994).

15. Restructuring effects between grades 8 and 10 are reported in Lee and Smith (1994, 1995). Effects between grades 10 and 12 are reported in Lee, Smith, and Croninger (1995).

16. Only in mathematics and science did NELS survey items about instruction from teachers and students offer useful indicators of some of the standards for authentic pedagogy as defined by CORS. The study is summarized in Lee, Smith, and Croninger (1995).

17. The study is based on a sample of 9,631 seniors in 789 high schools. An "average" student was defined as one who scored at the mean of eighth-grade achievement and mean socioeconomic status. Levels of authentic instruction were defined as follows: low = school that scored 1 standard deviation (SD) below the mean on authentic pedagogy for all schools; average = school that scored at the mean on authentic pedagogy for all schools; high = school that scored 1 SD above the mean on authentic pedagogy for all schools. Estimates of the effects of instruction represent an average effect across "average" students of different gender, race, or ethnic background.

The effects of school average authentic instruction appeared after taking into account effects on academic performance attributable to students' minority status, gender, SES, 8th-grade achievement, 8th-grade engagement in school, the number of academic courses they took in mathematics and science, the average SES of the school, level of minority enrollment in the school, whether the school was Catholic, whether the school was a private independent school, the size of student enrollment at the school, and the following aspects of school organization: average number of mathematics and science courses taken, variability in number of mathematics and sciences courses taken; variability in authentic instructional practices; collective responsibility and academic press.

These numbers represent gain scores, not fixed levels of achievement. Also, due to the measurement procedure of the NELS study, the gain scores do not represent points or questions answered correctly on a test, but a scale score derived from Item Response Theory (IRT). For mathematics, the actual range of scores on the final test was 16.77 to 78.28, and for science it was 10.03 to 35.96.

18. After controlling for social background, we found that authentic pedagogy was somewhat more likely to be experienced by students who had scored higher on conventional NAEP tests. The conclusions in this section on equity from the SRS are based on Newmann, Marks, and Gamoran (1995) and Marks, Newmann, and Gamoran (in press).

19. Authentic pedagogy did have more beneficial impact for students who scored higher on NAEP baseline achievement measures, but after this was considered, social background did not affect the achievement benefits of authentic pedagogy.

20. Conclusions from NELS on equity are presented in Lee and Smith (1994, 1995) and Lee, Smith, and Croninger (1995).

21. Lee, Bryk, and Smith (1993) provided a summary of research on the influence of organizational features of schools.

22. These findings are summarized in Louis, Kruse, and Marks (in press) and Marks, Secada, and Doane (in press). More detailed findings are presented in Louis, Marks, and Kruse (1995).

23. Support for student learning was measured both as students' perceptions of the general school environment and the amount of support and help for learning they experienced in a specific classroom.

24. An average student was one with the mean score on the NAEP measure of prior achievement and the mean score on socioeconomic status in the SRS sample, controlling for gender, race, and ethnicity. Levels of professional community were defined as follows: low = 1 standard deviation (SD) below the mean of SRS schools on professional community; average = mean on professional community; high = 1 SD above the mean of SRS schools on professional community. An average student in the low community school would score at the 36th percentile and in the high community school at the 67th percentile.

25. Achievement in the NELS:88 study was measured through items taken from

tests in the National Assessment of Educational Progress (NAEP). All results summarized here are presented in Lee, Smith, and Croninger (1995).

26. If the school average number of mathematics and science courses is high and if most students take the same number of courses (i.e., low variability), this is an indicator of consensus in the school that all students should study academically rigorous material. The analysis called special attention to achievement in mathematics and science, because only in these subjects did survey items from teachers and students offer useful indicators of some of the standards for authentic pedagogy.

27. Levels of common curriculum were defined as follows: low = 1 standard deviation (SD) below the mean on average number of mathematics and science courses taken and 1 SD above the mean in variability of mathematics and science course taking within the school; average = mean on average number of mathematics and science courses taken and mean variability in course taking; high = 1 SD above the mean on average number of mathematics and science courses taken and 1 SD below the mean in variability of mathematics and science course taking within the school. Individual and contextual variables included in this analysis are those indicated in note 17, but the level of authentic instructional practices in mathematics and science was also included here.

28. Effects of collective responsibility on achievement gains in all four subjects were found between grades 8 and 10 (Lee & Smith, in press). Effects on history and reading were not estimated for grades 10 and 12 (Lee, Smith, & Croninger, 1995), because the follow-up reported here included analysis of the effects of instructional practices, and adequate measures of these were not available for reading and history instruction.

School levels of collective responsibility were defined as follows: low = 1 standard deviation (SD) below the mean on collective responsibility for all schools; average = the mean on collective responsibility for all schools; high = 1 SD above the mean on collective responsibility for all schools. Individual and contextual variables included in this analysis are those indicated in note 17, but the level of authentic instructional practices in mathematics and science was also included here.

29. School levels of academic press were defined as follows: low = 1 standard deviation (SD) below the mean on academic press for all schools; average = mean on academic press for all schools; high = 1 SD above the mean on academic press for all schools. Individual and contextual variables included in this analysis are those indicated in note 17, but the level of authentic instructional practices in mathematics and science was also included here. We have no explanation for why the effects of academic press were much lower (and statistically not significant) in mathematics.

30. The percent advantages were computed by subtracting the gain in the lower schools from the gain in the higher schools, dividing this difference by the gain in the lower schools and multiplying by 100.

31. Louis, Kruse, and Marks (in press); Louis, Marks, and Kruse (1995).

32. Lee and Smith (in press).

33. Louis, Kruse, and Marks (in press). Louis, Marks, and Kruse (1995) discuss how high levels of human resources can compensate for the difficulties of building community in some large schools.

34. Sebring et al. (1995).

35. Regardless of the effect of size on professional community, smaller high schools are both more effective and more equitable in enhancing student achievement (Lee & Smith, 1994, 1995; Lee, Smith, & Croninger, 1995).

36. King, Louis, Marks, and Peterson (in press); Louis, Kruse, and Associates (1995).

37. Bryk, A. S., Easton, J. Q., Kerbow, D., Rollow, S. G., and Sebring, P. A. (1993).

38. Louis, Marks, and Kruse (1995); Lee and Smith (in press).

39. This analysis is based on and elaborated in Wehlage, Osthoff, and Porter (in press).

40. Bryk, A. S., Easton, J. Q., Kerbow, D., Rollow, S. G., and Sebring, P. A. (1993).

41. The account of Alexander is adapted from a more detailed version by Rollow and Bryk (1995).

42. Bryk, A. S., Easton, J. Q., Kerbow, D., Rollow, S. G., and Sebring, P. A. (1993, in preparation); Sebring et al. (1995).

43. In the School Restructuring Study, the most impressive examples of this occurred in schools of choice or magnet schools. The Chicago study found that social trust among teachers and between teachers and parents was a key factor associated with school improvement (Sebring et al., 1995). Distinctions among symbolic and substantive, consensual and conflictual parent involvement are explained by Wehlage, Osthoff, and Porter (in press).

44. Bryk, A. S., Easton, J. Q., Kerbow, D., Rollow, S. G., and Sebring, P. A. (in preparation).

45. Most of the stories of schools low in human resources that have "turned around" can be attributed to exceptionally effective principals who were given the authority to start special programs, usually with the authority to hire new staff. But when a school gets an effective principal with power to hire new staff, this immediately elevates the level of human resources, and the scenario becomes less convincing as an example of developmental success for a low resource school.

REFERENCES

Berends, M., & King, M. B. (1994). A description of restructuring in nationally nominated schools: Legacy of the iron cage? *Educational Policy, 8*(1), 28-50.

Bryk, A. S., Easton, J. Q., Kerbow, D., Rollow, S. G., & Sebring, P. A. (1993). *A view from the elementary schools: The state of reform in Chicago.* Chicago: Consortium on Chicago School Research.

Bryk, A. S., Easton, J. Q., Kerbow, D., Rollow, S. G., & Sebring, P. A. (in preparation). *Democratic participation and organizational change: The Chicago school experience.* Boulder, CO: Westview Press.

Bryk, A. S., Easton, J. Q., Rollow, S. G., & Sebring, P. A. (1994). The state of Chicago school reform. *Phi Delta Kappan, 76*(1), 74-78.

Bryk, A. S., & Rollow, S. G. (1992). The Chicago experiment: Enhanced democratic participation as a lever for school improvement. *Issue Report No. 3* (pp. 3-8). Madison, WI: Center on Organization and Restructuring of Schools.

King, M. B., Louis, K. S., Marks, H. M., & Peterson, K. D. (in press). Participatory decision making (Chapter 9). In F. M. Newmann & Associates, *School restructuring and student learning.* San Francisco: Jossey Bass.

Kruse, S. D. (1994). Redwood Valley Middle School: Shared leadership. In J. M. Jenkins, K. S. Louis, H. J. Walberg, & J. W. Keefe (Eds.), *World class schools: An evolving concept* (pp. 54-61). Reston, VA: National Association of Secondary School Principals.

Kruse, S., & Louis, K. S. (1995). Teacher teaming - Opportunities and dilemmas. *Brief to Principals,* No. 11. Madison, WI: Center on Organization and Restructuring of Schools.

Kruse, S., Louis, K.S., & Bryk, A. (1994). Building professional community in schools. *Issue Report No. 6* (pp. 3-6). Madison, WI: Center on Organization and Restructuring of Schools.

Lee, V., Bryk, A., & Smith, J. (1993). The organization of effective secondary schools. *Review of Research in Education, 19,* 171-267.

Lee, V. E., & Smith, J. (1993). Effects of school restructuring on the achievement and engagement of middle grade students. *Sociology of Education, 66*(3), 164-187.

Lee, V. E., & Smith, J. (1994). High school restructuring and student achievement: A new study finds strong links. *Issue Report No. 7* (pp. 1-11). Madison, WI: Center on Organization and Restructuring of Schools.

Lee, V. E., & Smith, J. (1995). Effects of high school restructuring and size on gains in achievement and engagement for early secondary school students. *Sociology of Education,* 68(4), 241-270.

Lee, V. E., & Smith, J. (in press). Collective responsibility for learning and its effects on gains in achievement and engagement for early secondary school students. *American Journal of Education.*

Lee, V. E., Smith, J., & Croninger, R. (1995). Another look at high school restructuring. Issues in *Restructuring Schools, No. 9.* Madison, WI: Center on Organization and Restructuring of Schools.

Louis, K. S., & King, J. K. (1993). Developing professional community: Does the myth of Sisyphys apply? In J. Murphy & P. Hallenger (Eds.), *Restructuring schools: Learning from ongoing efforts.* Newbury Park, CA: Corwin.

Louis, K. S., Kruse, S., & Associates (Eds.). (1995). *Professionalism and community: Perspectives on reforming urban schools.* Thousand Oaks, CA: Corwin.

Louis, K. S., Kruse, S. D., & Marks, H. M. (in press). School-wide professional community: Teachers' work, intellectual quality and commitment (Chapter 10). In F. M. Newmann & Associates, *School restructuring and student learning.* San Francisco: Jossey Bass.

Louis, K. S., Marks, H. M., & Kruse, S. (1995). *Teachers' professional community in restructuring schools.* Madison, WI: Center on Organization and Restructuring of Schools.

Lynn, L. (1994). Professional community - three case studies. *Issue Report No. 6* (pp. 7-16). Madison, WI: Center on Organization and Restructuring of Schools.

Marks, H. M., Newmann, F. M., & Gamoran, A. (in press). Does authentic pedagogy increase student learning? (Chapter 3). In F. M. Newmann & Associates, *School restructuring and student learning.* San Francisco: Jossey Bass.

Marks, H. M., Secada, W. G., & Doane, K. (in press). Student community (Chapter 11). In F. M. Newmann & Associates, *School restructuring and student learning.* San Francisco: Jossey Bass.

National Commission on Excellence in Education. (1983). *A nation at risk.* Washington, DC: U.S. Government Printing Office.

Newmann, F. M. (1991). What is a "restructured" school? A framework to clarify means and ends. *Issue Report No. 1.* Madison, WI: Center on Organization and Restructuring of Schools.

Newmann, F. M. & Associates (in press). *School restructuring and student learning.* San Francisco: Jossey Bass.

Newmann, F. M., Marks, H. M., & Gamoran, A. (1995). Authentic pedagogy: Standards that boost study performance. *Issues in Restructuring Schools No. 8.* Madison, WI: Center on Organization and Restructuring of Schools.

Newmann, F. M., Secada, W. G., & Wehlage, G. G. (1995). *A guide to authentic instruction and assessment: Vision, standards and scoring.* Madison, WI: Center on Organization and Restructuring of Schools.

Peterson, K. D., & Warren, V. D. (1994). Changes in school governance and principals' roles: Changing jurisdictions, new power dynamics and conflict in restructuring schools. In J. Murphy & K. S. Louis (Eds.), *Reshaping the principalship: Insights from transformational reform efforts* (pp. 219-235). Newbury Park, CA: Corwin.

Rollow, S., & Bryk, A. S. (1995). Catalyzing professional community in a school reform left behind. In K. S. Louis & S. D. Kruse (Eds.), *Professionalism and community: Perspectives on reforming urban schools* (pp. 105-132). Thousand Oaks, CA: Corwin.

Sebring, P. B., Bryk, A. S., Easton, J. Q., Luppescu, S., Thum, Y. M., Lopez, W. A., & Smith, B. S. (1995). *Charting reform: Chicago teachers take stock.* Chicago: Consortium on Chicago School Research.

Wehlage, G. G., Osthoff, E., & Porter, A. (in press). Support from external agencies. In F. M. Newmann & Associates, *School restructuring and student learning.* San Francisco: Jossey Bass.

APPENDIX: CENTER MISSION, STAFF, AND NATIONAL ADVISORY PANEL

Center Mission

The Center on Organization and Restructuring of Schools (CORS) studied how organizational features of schools can be changed to increase the intellectual and social competence of students. A five-year program of research focused on restructuring in four areas:

- The experiences of students in school.
- The professional life of teachers.
- The governance, management and leadership of schools.
- The coordination of community resources to better serve educationally disadvantaged students.

Through syntheses of previous research, analyses of existing data, and new empirical studies of education reform, the Center focused on six critical issues for elementary, middle and high schools:

- How can schooling nurture authentic forms of student achievement?
- How can schooling enhance educational equity?
- How can decentralization and local empowerment be constructively developed?
- How can schools be transformed into communities of learning?
- How can change be approached through thoughtful dialogue and support rather than coercion and regulation?
- How can the focus on student outcomes be shaped to serve these principles?

CORS RESEARCHERS AND SUPPORT STAFF

Lisa Byrd Adajian	Mary Jo Heck	Byong-Jin Park
John Balwit	Thomas Hoffer	Kent Peterson
Michael Bennett	Baesik Hong	Andrew Porter
Mark Berends	Daniel Hoover	Karen Prager
Patricia Berman	Christopher Jacobson	Diane Randall
Janet Bixby	Wayne Jennings	Mary Anne Raywid
Anthony Bryk	Lois Johnson	Pedro Reyes
Amy Cantoni	Jean Jolin	Mark Rigdon
Rudolfo Careago	M. Bruce King	Sharon Rollow
Courtney Cazden	Jean King	Sheila Rosenblum
David Chawszczewski	Sharon Kruse	David Scheer
Elizabeth Cohen	James Ladwig	Walter Secada
Jay Cradle	Valerie Lee	Laurie See
Robert Croninger	Paul LePore	Julia Smith
Paul Deabster	Pauline Lipman	Gregory Smith
Rhonda Dix	Virginia Long	BetsAnn Smith
Kenneth Doane	M. Peg Lonnquist	Corrine Solsrud
Eileen Ewing	Winifred Lopez	Deborah Stewart
Mary Fish	Karen Seashore Louis	Calvin Stone
Lorene Folgert	Sam Lucas	Vera Titunik
Michelle Foster	Leon Lynn	Valli Warren
Sherian Foster	Helen Marks	Gary Wehlage
Tae-joong Gahng	Norma Maynard	Matthew Weinstein
Adam Gamoran	Mary Morzinski	Julie White
Kubilay Gok	Fred Newmann	Stephen Witte
Dayle Hagland	Jean Norman	Carol Wright
Emily Hall	Martin Nystrand	Jung-Ho Yang
Donna Harris	Eric Osthoff	Maria Josefina Yanguas
Mary Hartzheim	Yuksel Ozden	Nicholas Young

NATIONAL ADVISORY PANEL

Richard C. Wallace, Jr. (Chair)
Professor
University of Pittsburgh
Pittsburgh, PA

Ronald J. Areglado
Director
National Principals Academy
National Association of
    Elementary School Principals
Alexandria, VA

Jomills Henry Braddock II
Professor
University of Miami
Coral Gables, FL

Ronald S. Brandt
Executive Editor
Journal of Educational Leadership
Association for Supervision and
    Curriculum Development
Alexandria, VA

Rueben A. Carriedo
Assistant Superintendent
San Diego City Schools
San Diego, CA

Larry Cuban
Professor
Stanford University
Palo Alto, CA

Sonia Hernandez
Policy Coordinator
California State Department
    of Education
Sacramento, CA

James W. Keefe
Director of Research
National Association
    of Secondary School Principals
Reston, VA

Ann Lieberman
Professor
Teachers College, Columbia
University
New York, NY

Milbrey W. McLaughlin
Professor
Stanford University
Palo Alto, CA

Yvonne A. Robinson
Gavin Elementary School
Chicago Heights, IL

Brian Rowan
Professor
University of Michigan
Ann Arbor, MI

Albert Shanker, President
Bella Rosenberg, Assistant to the
President
American Federation of Teachers
Washington, DC

Ron Anson *(ex officio)*
OERI Liaison
U.S. Department of Education
Washington, DC